BEYOND THE RELAXATION RESPONSE

D0888157

Also by Herbert Benson, M.D.

The Relaxation Response
The Mind/Body Effect

BEYOND THE RELAXATION RESPONSE

How to Harness the Healing Power of Your Personal Beliefs

by
Herbert Benson, M.D.
with William Proctor

𝕿imes
BOOKS

Published by TIMES BOOKS,
The New York Times Book Co., Inc.
130 Fifth Avenue, New York, N.Y. 10011

Published simultaneously in Canada by
Fitzhenry & Whiteside, Ltd., Toronto

Library of Congress Cataloging in Publication Data

Benson, Herbert.
  Beyond the relaxation response.

  Bibliography: p. 161
  Includes index.
  1. Mental healing. 2. Faith-cure. 3. Relaxation.
4. Medicine and psychology. I. Proctor, William. II. Title.
RZ401.B53 1984   616.8′51   83-45920
ISBN 0-8129-1107-5

Designed by Doris Borowsky

Manufactured in the United States of America

84 85 86 87 88 5 4 3 2 1

To Mother

Foreword

Since the writing of *The Relaxation Response* and *The Mind/Body Effect*, I have seen how the principles and practices presented in each can be combined successfully to bring about better health and well-being. The Relaxation Response when coupled with the power of belief can lead to remarkable health-promoting elements, which I have identified throughout as the Faith Factor. This new understanding has led to the publication of *Beyond the Relaxation Response*.

My work stands upon the shoulders of many observers and investigators who have contributed to the literature concerned with health and disease and with religion and belief. I have acknowledged their contributions when possible in the text and in the bibliography. In the text, case histories are presented. They are from either the medical literature or my own practice. My cases have all been altered so as to disguise the identity of the individual patients.

This book is not intended to give specific medical advice concerning personal health care. If the reader decides to use the principles of the book for the purpose of treating a specific medical problem, he or she should do so with the approval and subsequent supervision of his or her physician.

To avoid awkward sentence structures, the male gender has been used in most instances. I hope this does not offend.

I am very grateful to Claudia Dorrington, Nancy E. MacKinnon, Todd Moore, and Irene L. Goodale for their superb assistance in the preparation of this book. I also acknowledge the contributions of Jennifer C. Yolles, who indirectly aided this book by working on a related research project. For their counsel, I thank David M. Roseman, Robert E. Cowden, III, and Robert L. Allen. Once again, I am ever indebted to my wife, Marilyn, for her continued sound judgments, support, and patience.

Aspects of the book were made possible through funds given by The Ruth Mott Fund, the John E. Fetzer Foundation, William K. Coors, and the John D. and Catherine T. MacArthur Foundation. I also gratefully acknowledge the financial support given in honor of Pasquale and Lucy Pepe. The research and development of the book were also funded, in part, by grants from the United States Public Health Service (HL-22727 and HL-07374); from the National Science Foundation (NSF INT 8016982); and from the American Institute of Indian Studies.

—Herbert Benson, M.D.
December 1983

CONTENTS

PART ONE

An Introduction to the Power of the Faith Factor

1

IIIIIIIIIIIIIIIIIIIIIIIIIIIIIIIIII

What is the
Faith Factor?

IIIIIIIIIIIIIIIIIIIIIIIIIIIIIIIIII

When the film *Lawrence of Arabia,* the desert classic star-
ring Peter O'Toole, came out a number of years ago, there
were reports that concession stands were inundated at in-
termissions with demands for drinks—despite the fact that
many of the theaters were air-conditioned or in cool climates. A veritable epidemic of thirst hit many moviegoers
as they became immersed in the hot, sandy story they were
viewing on the screen.

The moral of this incident—and one of the major themes
of this book—is that the influential and even life-changing
forces we encounter are often not those things that are ex-
ternally real. In the case of *Lawrence,* of course, people
weren't really deprived of water, but they identified with
those waterless conditions so thoroughly that their bodies

became "convinced" they were on the Arabian dunes. The result: an overwhelming sense of thirst.

Medical and scientific research is demonstrating ever more clearly that the things we can touch, taste, and measure may frequently have to take a backseat to what we *perceive* or *believe* to be real. It's how we interpret reality, or how our body "sees" the concrete world around us, that is important. To put this another way, our personal powers and potential for well-being are shaped by the negative or positive ways we think. The first-century Roman philosopher Epictetus recognized this fact in this statement attributed to him: "Man is disturbed not by things, but by his opinion of things." In a similar vein, Proverbs 23:7 says of the person with an "evil eye," ". . . as he thinketh in his heart, so is he."

This principle of the importance of a person's personal beliefs has been one of the focal points of my own research during the years since the publication of *The Relaxation Response* in 1975 and *The Mind/Body Effect* in 1979. I've concluded after scientific observations conducted in the United States, the Indian Himalayas, and elsewhere that it's difficult to place definite limits on the physical and mental powers of those who hold profound beliefs.

My research has convinced me that there are many additional possibilities for the Relaxation Response—especially as it operates with a person's deepest religious or philosophical convictions—which were not apparent when my first two books were published. In my experience, those who discover the exciting and powerful forces of the mind do so by eliciting the Relaxation Response in conjunction with their personal belief system.

The term *Relaxation Response,* for those who may be unfamiliar with the concept, refers to the inborn capacity of

4

the body to enter a special state characterized by lowered heart rate, decreased rate of breathing, lowered blood pressure, slower brain waves, and an overall reduction of the speed of metabolism. In addition, the changes produced by this Response counteract the harmful effects and uncomfortable feelings of stress.

In this relatively peaceful condition, the individual's mental patterns change so that he breaks free of what I call "worry cycles." These are unproductive grooves or circuits that cause the mind to "play" over and over again, almost involuntarily, the same anxieties or uncreative, health-impairing thoughts.

Certain meditative and prayerful instructions can be employed to elicit the Relaxation Response. A simple technique I use to bring out the Relaxation Response in people is a four-step procedure that involves: (1) finding a quiet environment; (2) consciously relaxing the body's muscles; (3) focusing for ten to twenty minutes on a mental device, such as the word *one* or a brief prayer; and (4) assuming a passive attitude toward intrusive thoughts.

A number of years ago, I thought that this approach was all that was required to elicit benefits from the Relaxation Response. And it's true that the basic procedure is as valid as it ever was for helping individuals reduce stress, lower blood pressure, and otherwise enhance their physical and mental well-being. But now I've come to understand that the effects of this simple technique, *combined with a person's deepest personal beliefs,* can create other internal environments that can help the individual reach enhanced states of health and well-being.

This combination of a Relaxation-Response technique with the individual's belief system is what I call the "Faith Factor." It's by no means an entirely original concept;

rather, it's a new kind of "package" that contains two powerful but familiar spiritual vehicles: (1) meditation; and (2) a deeply held set of philosophical or religious convictions. My function in exploring and describing this Faith Factor is to serve, as best I can, as a bridge between two disciplines: traditional faith and meditative practices, and scientific observation.

I realize in stating this purpose that I'm embarking along a fine line that separates two conflicting ways of thinking—and that this combination may be potentially problematic. So, to make my task easier, I should mention here at the outset that in this book I'm not at all interested in promoting one religious or philosophical system over another. Nor do I intend to comment in any way on the truth or falsity of any religious system. Rather, I'm most concerned with the scientifically observable phenomena and forces that accompany faith. Also, I plan to concentrate on the techniques and attitudes that can be used by those of *any* faith to tap those forces.

More specifically, my research and that of others has disclosed that those who develop and use the Faith Factor effectively can:

- Relieve headaches
- Reduce angina pectoris pains and perhaps even eliminate the need for bypass surgery (an estimated 80 percent of angina pain can be relieved by positive belief!)
- Reduce blood pressure and help control hypertension problems
- Enhance creativity, especially when experiencing some sort of "mental block"
- Overcome insomnia
- Prevent hyperventilation attacks

- Help alleviate backaches
- Enhance the therapy of cancer
- Control panic attacks
- Lower cholesterol levels
- Alleviate the symptoms of anxiety that include nausea, vomiting, diarrhea, constipation, short temper, and inability to get along with others
- Reduce overall stress and achieve greater inner peace and emotional balance

This list could go on, but I think the principle is clear. Later, I'll describe in some detail how you can experience these and other physical and emotional improvements through some simple, practical Relaxation-Response techniques that are tailored to your own beliefs and value system. Whether you're sitting quietly in your room or jogging or swimming vigorously in the open air, there are ways you can plug into a beneficial realm of reality that we scientists are beginning to explore.

But let me offer some words of caution at this point. Despite the dramatic possibilities that can accompany the Faith Factor, I'm not suggesting that by following the procedures outlined in this book you can achieve perfect health or some sort of superhuman power over reality. In other words, this is not a blueprint to turn you into a superman or superwoman. Each of us is mortal and must operate within certain genetic limitations; this means every individual has a set ceiling for how far his mind or body will take him.

Furthermore, the Faith Factor should be used in conjunction with modern medicine. It should be an addition to the awesome cures that the medical profession can now perform and not a substitute for accepted medical care.

The two approaches—the Faith Factor *and* modern medicine—can enhance each other's impact and, together, bring about optimal results.

Having mentioned these qualifications, however, I'll also say that I believe most of us have little idea how great our individual potential or "performance ceiling" is, both physically and mentally. *If you truly believe in your personal philosophy or religious faith—if you are committed, mind and soul, to your world view—you may well be capable of achieving remarkable feats of mind and body that many only speculate about.*

So now, let me invite you to join in this quest to see just how far your mind—and your belief system, working through the channels of your mind—can take you. In the past, many have held out the promise of increasing the power of our minds and emotions over our bodies, and even over the outside world. It's the purpose of this book to bring some of this promise into reality.

2

‖‖‖‖‖‖‖‖‖‖‖‖‖‖‖‖‖‖‖‖‖

Frontiers of Scientific Research

‖‖‖‖‖‖‖‖‖‖‖‖‖‖‖‖‖‖‖‖‖

In recent years, certain explosive scientific theories have, in effect, been "blowing the lid" off our established ways of understanding reality. Of course, we do still accept many concepts and natural laws that have been around for centuries. For example, we know that by certain common measurements, a steel ball dropped from a building will fall at a certain accelerating rate of speed to the ground. We can also show in the laboratory that certain elements, such as hydrogen and oxygen, mixed in the right fashion, will produce another substance—in this case, water. Moreover, we know that specific antibiotic drugs will fight various infections effectively by destroying bacteria.

But some recent scientific developments have been turning other aspects of our thinking upside down. With Einstein's theory of relativity and the unified concepts of physics, what people once thought was real and comprehensible has changed dramatically. The steel ball that falls from a building is also plummeting through space in a different direction, as part of the solid matter on the earth, in the solar system, and in the galaxy. Not only that, the ball isn't really "solid" at all but consists of swirling atoms and molecules. And its very movement may be creating some invisible but real "waves" that change the arrangement of matter in other parts of the earth and the universe.

It's evident, then, that even though the old laws and concepts of the universe still have validity, they must now be understood in light of the new evidence and theories. Furthermore, these dramatic new scientific developments are also affecting our approach to the workings and capabilities of the human mind.

We must first question what is reality to our bodies. Is it what we see, hear, touch, and smell, or are there other realities that our senses cannot detect? Can our minds be altered by our *belief* in what is real? Do these altered states of mind then have the power to influence our health and well-being?

For example, we used to believe that there was a clearcut separation between outside forces and the direct reaction of the body to those forces. If you withheld water for a certain period of time from a person, he would get thirsty. Also, if you gave him water at regular intervals, he would remain satisfied. But as we saw in the previous chapter, the moviegoers who viewed the dry desert scenes in *Lawrence of Arabia* found that their consumption of water wasn't the only factor that determined thirst. Thirst, hunger, and a variety of other bodily reactions and powers depend not only on what is real, but also on what we *believe* to be real.

To illustrate this point further, let's consider two unusual ways in which the mind can have other dramatic effects on the body. First, we'll look at the impact of dreams, and then we'll explore the strange phenomenon of false pregnancy.

A medical researcher sixty years ago observed that most deaths occur around five or six o'clock in the morning. Also he found that during sleep, attacks of angina pectoris (chest pain related to a form of heart disease) were closely associated with "disturbed sleep." Later studies have confirmed these observations and tied in sleeping-angina problems, some of which may lead to death, with dreaming.

Specifically, Dr. J. B. Nowlin and his associates, using EKG equipment and other sophisticated monitoring devices to record the electrical activity of the heart and the brain, studied the relationship between measurable aspects of angina pectoris and REM (rapid eye movement) sleep, which is usually associated with dreaming. They discovered that "the general characteristics of the dreams which preceded an awakening with chest pain tended to fall into two broad categories: (1) those involving strenuous physical activity; and (2) those involving the emotions of fear, anger or frustration."

Of course, there are instances of anginal attacks during sleep when the person is not dreaming. But there is a persuasive body of evidence that indicates dreaming may in many cases trigger anginal pain. Why should this be? The obvious explanation is that during dreaming our minds "believe" that what we're dreaming about is actually happening, and our bodies respond accordingly. If we run in our dreams, we experience the physical effect of running in our bodies, even as we lie asleep. The results may be those of overexertion and pain, even though we've never left our beds.

Dreaming also has been associated with increased rates of gastric—or stomach—acid-secretion in patients with duodenal ulcers. In one study, Dr. R. H. Armstrong and his colleagues reported that in four of five patients significant increases in the rates of acid-secretion occurred during periods of dreaming. Armstrong concluded: "Many, but not all, dreams of duodenal ulcer patients evoke significant increases in secretion rate. Never were significantly increased rates seen in the absence of dreaming."

Another phenomenon that suggests a strong link between belief and bodily reactions is "pseudocyesis," a condition in which a woman believes herself to be pregnant and then develops many of the signs and symptoms of pregnancy. It's been referred to as the "oldest known psychosomatic condition." In fact, in 300 B.C. Hippocrates reported twelve cases of women "who imagine they are pregnant seeing that the menses are suppressed and the matrices swollen." In the sixteenth century, Mary Tudor recurrently experienced this phenomenon with symptoms of pregnancy that lasted nine months and culminated in two episodes of false labor.

This same experience of false pregnancy occurs today. Menstrual disturbances and abdominal enlargement occur at a rate similar to that of a normal pregnancy, and there may also be breast changes, including an increase in size, tenderness, the development of pigmentation, an increase in the size of papillae, and the secretion of milk. Some women have even experienced sensations of fetal movement during the fourth or fifth month. In fact, the symptoms of some patients were so convincing that nine of twenty-seven patients reported by one team of researchers were told by sixteen of forty examining physicians that they were pregnant. One case has even been reported in a male.

The precise causes of this condition aren't clear, but a number of explanations have been suggested: for example, psychological factors such as fear of pregnancy or an intense desire to have a child. Sometimes, the key ingredient giving rise to this condition has been thought to be depression, which may arise from a failed romance or the inability to have children. The resulting hormonal changes are believed to involve the pituitary gland and the hypothalamus, another area of the brain.

So from what we know about the effect of the mind on the body during dreams or in a condition like false pregnancy, it's evident that some powerful forces of personal belief are at work. The heart, stomach, and uterus are rather "dumb" in the sense they have no eyes or ears. Consequently, they are to a large extent dependent upon the messages they receive from the brain. Reality for our organs can be what the mind *perceives* as reality and then transmits in physical messages to them.

One way to understand how the brain can create reality is to imagine that the billions of cells in the brain are part of circuits that are not yet connected. In effect, they need to be "wired." Every time we experience or learn something new, additional wiring is put into place. If a child is taught that two plus two equals four, and if she is given the opportunity to practice that simple addition a few times with apples, oranges, and other familiar objects, the wires for that bit of knowledge will be connected. She won't have to relearn that information again every time she wants to use it; she'll simply employ her newly created mental circuit or pathway.

Herbert Benson, M.D.

There are many factors that influence the creation of these new pathways. These include genetic makeup, the stage of development of our nervous systems, the influence of our environment, and our health. The list can go on, but the point is that our brains can create new circuits or wirings that contain new information. As we get older, it's more difficult for many of us to develop new circuits and to learn as quickly as when we were younger. If disease develops, such as a stroke or hardening of the arteries of the brain, some of the previously intact circuits may be destroyed, and we forget things.

Of course, any analogy has weaknesses, especially when you're dealing with something as complex as the human brain. As a result, talking about wires in your head, which carries the connotation of ordinary electrical circuits or even something as advanced as man-made computers, isn't quite adequate. It's true that electrical impulses play an important role in the thinking process, but so do chemicals called neurotransmitters. Moreover, the computer analogy falls short because human mental activity occurs with the simultaneous, parallel movement of various impulses. Computers, in contrast, for the most part work on a linear principle, with one set of computations leading directly to another.

With these qualifications in mind let's stick with the wiring image for the time being because it's helpful in understanding unusual potentials of the mind. The mental wires help make up the network of what we know as our memories, and memory may intrude in disturbing, uninvited ways into our lives. To illustrate, take the case of a response that your body may have "learned" as a result of some past experience. Suppose, for instance, that at some time in the past you ate a piece of food with a distinctive odor, which

14

made you violently ill. As a result, you have come to associate the smell with the illness. In the future, it would be possible just for the smell of that food to make you nauseous or even cause you to vomit again—even though you may never actually eat the food.

What's happened here is that your brain has been reminded by the distinctive odor, which triggers the response of nausea and vomiting. The actual intake of the food into your stomach isn't necessary. The circuits in your brain are already complete, with appropriate wires in place, and the smell is all that's needed.

A similar physical response might occur, as we've already seen, from dreaming. You might wake up sweating with a pounding heart after having a dream that involved memories or thoughts that had been previously wired into your brain. Because these wired thoughts are incomplete, dreams have a fragmentary nature and may go on for only a brief time. But for your organs, the impression of reality of even a very short dream may be enough to cause dramatic changes in your body. In other words, as far as your body is concerned, what's going on in your mind during that dream *is* real.

The mind's influence over your body in these powerful subconscious ways can be positive as well as negative. Those wires that have been developing in your brain can make you feel good as well as bad. So, you can walk into a flower-filled room and be overwhelmed with the airy, springlike smells—only to learn later that the flowers are made of plastic or silk.

The power the mind can exercise over the body and the five senses becomes important when medical treatment is involved. Suppose that a person is prescribed a drug to treat tension and nervousness. He is told by his doctor to keep the pills with him at all times, but to take them only when he feels he has his bothersome symptoms. The person does in fact take the drug a few times and feels noticeably better.

With time, the patient finds that just having the drug with him is enough to keep him calm, and as a result he rarely has to take it. When he begins to feel tense, he just thinks about taking the drug that is available in his pocket, and this knowledge is often enough to activate the circuits in his brain, resulting in the relief the pill would have given him. In this case, the tension the patient feels is very real, and it produces nervousness. Furthermore, the patient found the drug was effective in countering his symptoms, and his confidence in the drug increased with each use. But soon, all he needed was the *faith* that the drug would eliminate the tension. His mind began to do the work of the drug. In fact, in many research studies, individuals with diverse symptoms who have been given a nonmedicated pill, or placebo, have gotten well as quickly as other people do with medication.

In a similar kind of situation, there is the man who visits his doctor because he "doesn't feel well." After taking his medical history, performing a physical examination, and obtaining laboratory tests, the doctor may be unable to detect anything measurably wrong. He then reassures his patient that the bad feeling will soon pass—perhaps because there's a temporary virus or bacterium that's been prevalent. The patient leaves the office in a better frame of mind, and soon he finds he's feeling well again.

In this case, the doctor didn't prescribe anything. Instead, he did something that may have been even more important: By his reassuring manner, he stimulated certain circuits of experience in the patient's mind, circuits that signaled nothing was really wrong and the bad feelings were inappropriate.

In medical parlance, this type of incident is often referred to as the "placebo effect." The doctor's verbal assurances and comforting manner, which conveyed his beliefs, interacted with beliefs of the patient and, without any specific medical intervention, caused detectable physiological changes. The patient trusted the doctor and placed his faith in the doctor's ability to make him well. To return to our wiring analogy, those circuits or "loops" in the brain were rerouted by the patient's belief in the doctor and in modern medicine's diagnostic abilities, and as a result the symptoms disappeared.

Of course, if something had been seriously wrong with this man or with anyone else, it might not have been enough for the doctor to be reassuring. Medications or surgical operations have to be used in many situations. Of all the patients who see their doctors, however, it's been estimated that 75 percent have conditions that will eventually get better by themselves, if they get better at all. For such illnesses, there are no specific treatments. The remaining 25 percent represent specific illnesses that can be diagnosed by modern medicine and that can often be treated with awesome success. On the other hand, the power and potential of the placebo effect—and all the similar relationships of the mind to the body—assume a role of primary importance in many of the 75 percent of health problems that don't respond to specific treatments. Moreover, even in the other 25 percent, the medical treatments may be enhanced by the placebo effect.

In attempting to learn the full role the brain plays in alleviating or aggravating symptoms and diseases, we now recognize that the power of the mind must never be dismissed. We know that *any* treatment is more likely to be successful if the patient has a great deal of faith in his physician's ability—or even faith that a higher spiritual power is at work in his body. For example, high blood pressure, headaches, and even alleged terminal illness have been healed without any identifiable medical treatment. The only thing that seemed to make a difference was the patient's deep belief that he could be cured.

How far can the mind go in acting on the body? Also, if the mind has such powerful properties, what are the means or tools that will enable you to maximize your mental powers?

One approach to understanding the vast possibilities of personal belief for our mental powers is to return to those scientific advances in medicine, physics, and other disciplines mentioned at the beginning of this chapter. On one level, the action of our minds on our bodies must certainly be physical. In other words, our brains are tremendously complex and have great potential for triggering dramatic reactions elsewhere in our bodily system. Those electrical impulses and neurotransmitters in our minds can make us thirsty when we don't really need any water; they may cause our bodies to be healed when modern medicine can give no explanation for the healing; and they can produce tranquil or tumultuous emotions, even when there seems to be no objective, outward reason for such reactions.

Is it possible, however, that the action of our minds also influences things *outside* our bodies? Can our minds somehow create—or participate in creating—rippling disturbances in the universe that can alter not only our own bodies but also the physical surroundings outside our bodies? For some, such thoughts are the stuff of science fiction. For others, on the other hand, these considerations suggest the merging of scientific and theological thinking.

The theoretical physicists who are exploring "unified theories" of matter and energy suspect that there is a single force that underlies all the physical reality in the universe. They suggest that in the very beginning all the protons, neutrons, and various subatomic particles and energy waves that have proliferated throughout our galaxies and make up the underpinnings of physical reality were one. Even today these particles and waves bear the imprint of that one primordial force and can only be fully understood in terms of the fundamental, unified relationship they have with one another.

In the branch of physics known as quantum mechanics, scientists have suggested various explanations or theories about the fundamental nature of all matter. Our world, they say, can be broken down into atoms and molecules, which can in turn be divided still further into "subatomic particles" and energy waves. These particles and waves are everywhere and in everything; also, the particles can't be said to exist as tangible objects occupying space. Rather, they might be viewed as fundamental forces or sets of movements. To put it more accurately, the particles aren't really "particles" at all in the way we normally think of that term: They are really a set of *relationships* between particles and waves that can't be described or visualized in our ordinary thought processes.

These subatomic particles and waves don't exist in isolation. They are interdependent and react constantly with one another. In fact, according to those who believe in the possibility of a "superunified theory" of the universe, all things arose out of one entity or force and can only be understood in terms of the fundamental, unified relationship they have with one another.

One expression of this concept, as Gary Zukav indicates in *The Dancing Wu Li Masters,* is known as "Bell's theorem." The physicist J. S. Bell in 1964 said, in a complex mathematical formula, that at the most profound level the various subatomic particles and waves in the universe are intimately connected.

It's at this point that physics and religious thought begin to merge: Theoretical thinkers in theologies as divergent as Buddhism and Christianity have, in other terminology, affirmed just such a unified theory of the universe.

Many Buddhists, for example, believe that there is a profound connection or force that binds together all things—people, trees, rocks, and animals. When a person meditates or prays, they believe he is tapping into that basic force. And in entering into this fundamental energy field, Buddhists believe, we can become imbued with powers far beyond the scope of normal human achievements.

For example, Tibetan Buddhists have claimed to be able to melt the snow around them by generating heat during meditation. They have also claimed it's possible to defy the forces of gravity by flying through the air—just by putting one's mind in a profound harmony with the deepest forces and structures of reality. In other words, these Buddhists are affirming in religious terms a "unified theory" of reality, in which mind and body become one with outside physical phenomena to produce highly unusual results.

A similar kind of thinking may be found among some Christian theologians, who have worked to incorporate into their beliefs the theories of Einstein and various other contemporary concepts of physics. One of the most imaginative of these thinkers is Thomas F. Torrance, formerly professor of Christian Dogmatics at the University of Edinburgh and a winner of the prestigious Templeton Foundation Prize for progress in religion. Torrance notes that the old language of physics, which emphasized that matter was made up only of disparate particles, has had to give way in recent years to unified theories, stressing the connections between the most basic forms of subatomic waves, particles, and forces. Furthermore, he argues that Einstein's language of relativity and the concepts of later theoretical physicists should be applied to Christian theology. In particular, in his book *Space, Time and Incarnation,* he outlines his goal of setting forth a unitary approach to Christ's incarnation.

He writes that Christ's incarnation—or the appearance of the eternal, timeless God in human form—is an expression of the basic unity in the universe, the oneness between God and his creation. "Jesus Christ is the place of contact and communication between God and man. . . ." The "place" in the universe that Jesus occupied ". . . is filled with the energy of divine being and life, but . . . also filled with the energy of human being and life."

Hence, Torrance says, we are confronted in the incarnation with a situation where we have to think things out in a "kinetic way," or in terms of the most basic movements and forces of an infinite God who can "locate Himself in our space and time as one with us." He also stresses that "the place of God in Jesus Christ must be an open concept, rooted in the space and time of this world yet open to the transcendent presence of God."

One of the problems of understanding concepts like the incarnation and the resurrection is that modern biology has not yet been able to formulate open-ended, unified concepts and terminology that suggest subatomic ties with the other sciences. As a result, Torrance says, it's difficult to understand the resurrection from the dead in biological terms. We simply don't have the human language or symbols to describe a physical entry or intrusion by supernatural or extra-dimensional forces into our three-dimensional realm of space and time.

It's necessary, he explains, to penetrate "into connections that are real although they can have no direct correspondence to our observational experience." And it's also essential to understand "that a different kind of structure, that of space-time, is required if we are to think out the interrelatedness of things in the cosmos." The basic message of many religious documents—including the Old and New Testaments—is that a being or beings from an extra-dimensional reality have revealed something of their realm to three-dimensional human beings. And religious faith, according to the Bible, is a force that triggers the interactions between our universe and the "universe" of God.

It's important to recognize throughout these abstract, theoretical discussions that Torrance has a very "high" view of Scripture. That is, he accepts the historical and miraculous accounts as substantially accurate as they are presented. Furthermore, he rejects the attempts by Rudolph Bultmann and other theologians to "demythologize" the Bible, or strip it of its literally supernatural elements.

Also, Torrance is *not* saying that if we just come up with the right theories and scientific language, we'll be able to explain and understand completely who God is and what he has done in the world. The entire truth of those supernatural events must remain, in the last analysis, beyond human understanding: The supernatural is rooted in a higher, extradimensional form of reality—a reality that extends

beyond our limited human faculties of perception and intel-
lect. Divine revelation, or breakthroughs from the higher
reality to our own, must ultimately determine what we can
know of God and the supernatural realm.

On the other hand, Professor Torrance does believe that
the language of theoretical physics can help us understand a
little better what happened during such events as the incarnation and the resurrection. The reason we can understand
and experience this more fundamental reality is that in
some sense it's always here with us, always available to interact with us.

At this point we find ourselves returning to some of the
more advanced thought of Buddhism. Certainly, there is a
world of difference between the paths to salvation presented by Buddhists and many Christian thinkers. But still,
there does seem to be a significant overlap between the way
Buddhists, theologians like Torrance, and modern theoretical physicists approach the real underlying nature of the
physical world. The Buddhists, as Gary Zukav points out in
The Dancing Wu Li Masters, believe that the human who
reaches a state of "enlightenment" succeeds in transcend-
ing ordinary logical thought and perceiving directly "the in-
expressible nature of undifferentiated reality."

The unenlightened person sees the physical world as
many separate parts, Zukav notes. In contrast, for the en-
lightened Buddhist, "These separate parts . . . are not
really separate. According to mystics from around the
world, each moment of enlightenment (grace/insight/
samadhi/*satori*) reveals that everything—all the separate
parts of the universe—are manifestations of the same
whole. There is only *one* reality, and it is whole and unified. It is one."

The concept of unity also connects metaphysics with

modern physics, Zukav says: "In short, both in the need to cast off ordinary thought processes (and ultimately to go 'beyond thought' altogether) and in the perception of reality as one unity, the phenomenon of enlightenment and the science of physics have much in common."

What does all this have to do with the way our minds may affect our bodies and our physical environment?

A possible connection lies in this direction:

If the universe is indeed interconnected, we may be able to learn how to use our minds to understand and perhaps influence the reality outside our bodies. Then, we might greatly expand our control not only over our bodies but also over the physical reality around us.

I came to these considerations through my study of the Relaxation Response. In my earlier books, I described the Relaxation Response as a bodily reaction brought on by relaxational and meditative techniques that anyone can employ to strip away destructive inner stresses. These techniques cause scientifically measurable changes to occur in your body: Metabolism and heart and respiration rates decrease; alpha wave output of the brain is intensified; and a general calming effect ensues. By eliciting this bodily response, millions of people have trained themselves to call forth, on demand, a healthful, calming effect in their bodies.

I learned after performing this early research and writing these books that the Relaxation Response had served as the basic introduction in cultures throughout the world to the potential powers that are at our disposal. In short, many claimed that for those who combine the Relaxation Response with a deep personal faith, the limits of personal power over the physical world could be expanded greatly. Moreover, the verification of such powers was in many cases within the realm of measurement. After all, Tibetan Buddhists had been reported to be able to stay alive in mid-winter without clothes by employing a form of meditation that was rooted in a profound religious faith. If they could really accomplish this feat, surely Western scientists could observe and monitor the event with the proper equipment.

PART TWO

AN ADVENTURE IN THE HIMALAYAS

3

The Road to Upper Dharmsala

Old-fashioned adventures to unknown regions of the earth, "lost" continents, or lands with strange, exotic people are few and far between these days. But the desire to explore a new frontier or discover an entirely new civilization is still deeply imbedded in human aspirations.

I count myself lucky to have had an opportunity recently to lead a group of scientists on an old-fashioned expedition. The frontiers I wanted to explore encompassed many of the mind-body possibilities that fascinated me as I worked at Boston's Beth Israel Hospital and at the Harvard Medical School. The expedition I hoped to organize would involve travel to an out-of-the way-region in the Indian Himalayas. I wanted to delve into spiritual practices and mind-body feats that most Westerners only mentioned in terms of legend or superstition—things like raising skin temperatures to incredible heights; causing the body to fly or "levitate" at will; and even moving objects with a kind of mental force field. In short, I wanted to study what might be called the "outer limits" of the supernormal abilities claimed by such spiritual explorers as the Buddhist monks of Tibet: I wanted to test scientifically their claims that through deep meditation they could influence their bodies and the surrounding physical world with their minds.

Of course, the Tibetan Buddhists are certainly not the only Buddhists practicing meditation; nor are Buddhists the only religious people who meditate. Many of the same techniques—though not the same spiritual content—are employed by meditators from Christian, Jewish, Hindu, and other traditions. But the Tibetan Buddhists are known for their meditative techniques perhaps more than any other practitioners of mysticism, and some of their extraordinary claims about increased skin heat and levitation were tantalizing to me.

For example, Alexandra David-Neal relates ancient accounts like these in *Magic and Mystery in Tibet:*

. . . I could clearly see his perfectly calm impassive face and the wide-open eyes with their gaze fixed on some invisible far-distant object situated somewhere high up in space. The man did not run. He seemed to lift himself from the ground, proceeding by leaps. It looked as if he had been endowed with the elasticity of a ball and rebounded each time his feet touched the ground. His steps had the regularity of a pendulum. . . .

Some initiates in the secret lore also assert that, as a

result of long years of practice, after he has travelled over a certain distance, the feet of the *lung-gom-pa* no longer touch the ground and that he glides on the air with an extreme celerity. . . .

A pit is dug in the ground, its depth being equal to the height of the candidate. Over the pit is built a kind of cupola whose height from the ground level to its highest point again equals that of the candidate. A small aperture is left at the top of the cupola. Now between the man seated cross-legged at the bottom of the pit and that opening, the distance is twice the height of his body. . . . The test consists in jumping cross-legged . . . and coming out through the small opening at the top of the cupola. I have heard Khampas declare this feat has been performed in their country, but I had not myself witnessed anything like it. . . .

The neophytes sit on the ground, cross-legged and naked. Sheets are dipped in the icy water, each man wraps himself in one of them and must dry it on his body. As soon as the sheet has become dry, it is again dipped in the water and placed on the novice's body to be dried as before. The operation goes on [in] that fashion until daybreak. Then he who has dried the largest number of sheets is acknowledged the winner of the competition.

Besides drying wet sheets on one's body, there exist various other tests to ascertain the degree of heat which the neophyte is able to radiate. One of these tests consists in sitting in the snow. The quantity of snow melted under the man and the distance at which it melts around him are taken as measures of his ability.

31

So the reports that had come out of Tibet were quite fascinating, and if true, they promised significant opportunities for making some new scientific measurements and findings. My decision to embark on this adventure was just the first small step toward my goal, however. Wanting to study the monks of Tibet is one thing, but *doing* so is quite something else. There are enormous political and practical obstacles that must be overcome before any expedition can get off the ground.

First of all, the monks are no longer actually in Tibet. When the Chinese Communists moved in during 1959, the practice of religion was outlawed. Thousands of religious people were jailed or executed. The number of Buddhist monasteries was reduced from more than twenty-four hundred to ten. The Dalai Lama, along with thousands of the religious and cultural elite, fled Tibet to India, where they were permitted to establish a government in exile. They settled in the small village known as Upper Dharmsala, on a plateau seven thousand feet above sea level in the Indian Himalayas.

Another problem is that most religious meditators see little value in testing their experience scientifically. They already know the inner and outer effects produced; nothing has to be proved to them. Also, because the various meditative rites are steeped in religious tradition, scientific observation may be regarded as a sacrilege. Various research attempts to validate the seemingly fantastic claims for meditation had been consistently discouraged in the past. The Yogis simply felt they were beyond worldly considerations, and they didn't feel a need to demonstrate their techniques to anyone. Often, it was impossible even to approach the Yogis or monks. They would retreat into their caves or hermitages whenever some inquirer appeared. Faced with such discouraging precedents, I was concerned that I might never find a group of experienced monks that I could test.

But there were several distinctive features about the Tibetan Buddhists that prompted me to pursue them as possible subjects. Their religious leader, His Holiness the Dalai Lama, whom the Tibetans consider to be the reincarnation of Buddha, is also the head of state. As the ultimate temporal *and* spiritual authority, he commanded exceptional obedience and respect. So there was little question that his disciples, who practiced advanced meditation under his guidance, would follow whatever directions he gave them. My task then was to try to get in touch with the Dalai Lama and convince him of the importance of my proposed mission.

When I learned that His Holiness would be touring the United States in 1979, I wrote his representative, Mr. Tenzin N. Tethong, in New York City to see if we could arrange a meeting. In my letter, I described my own interest and research in meditation and told him I'd like to have access to Tibetan Buddhist practitioners for research that could benefit many religious traditions. To my delight, Mr. Tethong soon replied that the Dalai Lama would be visiting Harvard on his tour, and it would be possible for me to meet with him for a half hour.

I began immediately to make preparations for this important audience. First of all, I assembled a small group of colleagues to accompany me—those who had worked with me or provided or offered support on various research projects. We met in the early afternoon on a sunny, mid-October day in the living room of the Dana-Palmer House, an 1823 building owned by Harvard University. William James had lived there, and it's the location where he's believed to have conceived his idea of a pluralistic universe.

At precisely the appointed time, the Dalai Lama's representatives filed into the room, and one of them reminded me that the meeting could last only half an hour—not a minute longer. Then, the Dalai Lama walked in, wearing his traditional crimson and golden robes. He's an average-sized man by Western standards, with a gentle Oriental face and features, and he seemed rather tired, probably because he was nearing the end of an exhausting tour.

Without fanfare, he sat down and began chatting pleasantly to me and my companions through his translator. He was curious about the precise purpose of the meeting, and I explained that we were doctors who had already conducted studies on meditation. Specifically, I said, we had learned that there are physiological changes in people who meditate.

"As a cardiologist, I deal with the effects of stress and its relation to heart disease," I explained. "We know that stress, through hypertension, may cause heart disease. But we've also discovered that people who practice a simple form of meditation can achieve profound physiological changes—including a reduction of hypertension. What I hope is that you'll allow us to study people who practice *advanced* meditation so that we can see how far these mind-body capacities may go."

Specifically, I said, we wanted to study *gTum-mo* Yoga—a practice by which the skin's temperature is supposed to increase significantly. We had heard that monks could cause their skin to become so hot that they could dry wet, icy garments that were draped around them. Also, we would be interested in meeting any monks who practiced *lung gom-pa* Yoga, part of which entailed the ability to levitate. Supposedly, those who can achieve this state are also able to transport themselves with "swift footedness" from boulder to boulder while hardly touching the ground.

"With our equipment, we can readily measure these feats scientifically," I told the Dalai Lama.

This information about our scientific methods seemed to arouse his interest. "You mean you measure actual physical changes within the body?" he asked—this time in English.

I assured him it would indeed be possible to do this under properly controlled conditions. But then he began to hedge a bit, and reverting to Tibetan, he presented the standard answer other researchers and I had heard for years: "It would be very difficult for these abilities to be measured. The people who practice this meditation do it for religious purposes. They must be experienced in order to feel the benefits. You *must* experience it first."

Well, I thought to myself, it was a good try. There was no way to argue him into accepting the validity of a scientific approach. Before I could get completely discouraged, though, he returned to English again and began to muse out loud: "Still, our culture is undergoing many changes. We have been forced out of our homeland into exile." He smiled and said, "Our 'friends' to the East [the Chinese] might be impressed with a Western explanation of what we are doing. Perhaps there is some worth in allowing this study to be done."

Apparently, the Dalai Lama viewed our proposal as a way to validate his religious practices to the Chinese, who had forced the monks to flee Tibet. With his culture and religious heritage in danger of dying out, the Dalai Lama saw our proposal as a way not only to document his faith's contributions but also perhaps even to help save it from possible extinction.

After a brief pause, he added with what seemed to be a rather wistful look: "Perhaps if I ask several people to be studied, they will allow it."

Now, I felt we were on our way. No Tibetan Buddhist should even consider refusing a request from the Dalai Lama. But before he would give his final approval, he asked that we also take a look at Tibetan medicine from the viewpoint of Western science. In particular, he said, "Pay attention to the three main components of Tibetan medicine—the belief of the doctor, the belief of the patient, and the *karma* between the two."

I burst out laughing. Then, in case he should take offense, I explained: "The reason I laugh is that those three elements you say are in your medicine are precisely what we call the 'placebo effect.' This phenomenon is something that we in the West are just beginning to appreciate fully, but apparently it's something you have known about and used for centuries."

Of course, I knew that his culture was lacking in the knowledge and practice of Western medicine: antibiotics, surgical procedures, and other recent scientific advances. But they *were* perhaps far ahead of us in understanding how mental activity and personal beliefs affect the body. As I had told him, the closest we could come to them in this area was our rudimentary knowledge of the placebo effect—or the combination of the belief of the doctor, the belief of the patient, and the joint forces released by their interacting beliefs and personalities (or the "karma," as the Dalai Lama had put it).

The session continued for more than an hour and a half. Before it was over, the Dalai Lama had indicated that he was now well aware of the work we had done in studying meditation. He also paid us a rare compliment—one which

I felt sealed our understanding that he would allow us to pursue our experiments among his people: "Your way of identifying the physiological impact of spiritual forces has done a thousand times more to bring the religions of the world together than all of the philosophers."

I was quite encouraged after this discussion had ended and we had gone our separate ways, but then several months passed without any word from the Dalai Lama. I began to wonder if he had forgotten about our meeting. Or worse, I wondered if he had changed his mind. After all, he had expressed misgivings at several points: The meditative techniques were considered to be private and secret matters. They supposedly gave human beings powers that went far beyond the normal sphere of human experience. As a general rule, a person had to be prepared for years before the powers could be imparted to him. If these secrets should fall into the hands of those who were "unenlightened," there was a potential that they could be used for evil.

As such thoughts began to bother me, I was on the verge of trying to contact him once again. But then a letter arrived from his office. He had found three people who were willing to be studied, and now all that remained was for me and my team to raise the funds to get there and conduct the experiments. So I wasted no time in making preparations and securing the necessary funding.

After months of searching, we finally pieced together funding for our trip from a variety of sources: the American Institute of Indian Studies, the National Science Foundation, the National Institutes of Health, the Fleishmann Foundation, and the John E. Fetzer Foundation. It had been a difficult job to get the money because our purpose defied the usual categories for government and foundation funding. We weren't strictly medical, anthropological, or religious; rather, we were a combination of these and other disciplines.

With the funds in hand, I assembled our travel party. In addition to myself, there was another physician-medical researcher, Dr. John W. Lehmann, who was a research fellow at Harvard and Beth Israel Hospital; Dr. Jeffrey Hopkins, the noted Tibetan-English translator who was director of the Center for South Asian Studies at the University of Virginia and who was also the translator at my original meeting with the Dalai Lama; and Mark D. Epstein, a Harvard medical student, and his wife, a photographer, Ellen Perlman.

Also, a free-lance filmmaker, Russell Pariseau, heard of the forthcoming trip only four weeks before departure. He asked to accompany us with his one assistant, Penny Cravens, at his own expense—even after I told him I had not secured permission to film the studies. Furthermore, I said, there was no time to get permission, and if a choice had to be made between the science and the film, the science would have priority. Still, he elected to take the chance.

Our choice of equipment was as important as our choice of personnel. The first person I went to see was my friend and colleague, Dr. Ralph F. Goldman, director of the Military Ergonomics Division of the U.S. Army Institute of Environmental Medicine, in Natick, Massachusetts. These laboratories specialize in testing human capacities in different environments, and I knew he had precisely the equipment we needed, including small disk thermometers called thermistors to make accurate measurements of the Tibetan monks' skin temperatures. Also, we secured specialized flexible rectal thermometers to measure inner body temperature. Finally, to complete the equipment necessary to measure the effect of *gTum-mo* Yoga on the body, Dr. Goldman supplied us with a mini weather station. With these devices, we could monitor the environmental temperature, relative humidity, wind speed, and radiant heat of the sun. We would then be able to calculate the various effects on body temperature.

Of course, we knew objections on the grounds of sacrilege might be raised against using any of this equipment on the meditating monks—and especially the rectal thermometers. For all we knew, they might even balk at our taking photographs. I had not asked any specific questions about these procedures earlier.

In February 1981, we boarded a Pan American flight heading directly to Delhi, India. From the moment I stepped onto the plane, I knew I was already involved with a radically different culture. There were many Moslems and Hindus on the flight, and as soon as we left sight of the American coast and headed out over the Atlantic, two Moslems started to argue gently about the direction in which their prayer rug should face. Upon arrival, my own Western mind-set gave me difficulty in getting perspective on many things about this Eastern culture. I saw hundreds—perhaps thousands—of homeless men and women suffering from malnutrition, and many had deformed bodies, the skin lesions of leprosy, and a variety of other physical disorders. Certainly I knew what could be done to help relieve these problems on a broad scale, but there were insufficient funds available to employ curative Western medical techniques. By most Western standards, Indian levels of care were backward. Still, here I was, in this same "backward" country, intending to study and learn some advanced techniques of mind-body interaction.

The irony of the situation was obvious. Gradually, though,

I came to realize that my sense of irony was a two-edged sword. Just as this culture had been slow to accept Western technological advances, so we had been slow to recognize *their* progress in the field of meditation. That was the main thing I had to keep in mind: I had come to this land to learn, not to criticize. The person who helped me most to make the transition to this new way of thinking was a man who joined our expedition in India, Dr. M. S. Malhotra, an internationally recognized Indian physiologist and director of N.S. (Netaji Subhas) National Institute of Sports in Patiala, India. This extraordinary scientist, who came along on the recommendation of Dr. Ralph Goldman, proved to be of inestimable value to our work—and also became my close friend.

As I tried to adjust to this society during the few days before we embarked on our trip to the Indian Himalayas, a relatively odd event occurred. The day before we left New Delhi, I set out walking alone on the streets near our hotel. Soon, I found myself in a café having a cup of tea. As I surveyed the other customers around me, I was astonished to see Dr. Robert Keith Wallace, my original collaborator years before in studying the physiological impact of meditation on members of the Transcendental Meditation movement. We had not seen each other for more than six years.

Although we had started experiments independently of one another, we had come to the same conclusion: There were measurable physiological changes that resulted from meditation. For a while, we joined to collate our data and publish our findings, but we later disagreed over the universality of the changes that could take place with different types of meditation, and so we parted ways. In short, he felt there was something unique about the techniques of Transcendental Meditation that caused the changes. I, on the other hand, believed the key physical changes could be elicited regardless of any particular meditation technique. Dr. Wallace went on to become the president of the Maharishi International University, and I continued my more general work on meditation at Harvard's Thorndike Memorial Laboratory and Boston's Beth Israel Hospital.

After I joined him that day in the New Delhi café, we spoke for some time and attempted to renew our friendship. He said he had come to India on business for the Maharishi Mahesh Yogi. Since I knew the TM movement was involved in levitation and other forms of advanced meditation, this chance encounter presented me with a great opportunity to get some additional background information for my own expedition. I had not been able to witness levitation even though I had asked periodically about it.

"Do people really levitate?" I asked him.

"Yes, you can get off the ground," he replied.

"Does anyone hover?"

"No," he said. "You're up and then you're down. In a sense, you 'think yourself light' through special mantras and get yourself up, and then you come down immediately."

"But things are being claimed . . ."

"It is *possible* to float—that has been done in the past, and it will be done in the future. But the Maharishi feels that the world isn't ready yet to accept such profound feats because of the general state of evil."

Hearing this qualification of things that had been claimed by other Eastern meditators, including the Tibetan Buddhists, made me wonder if what I was searching for was a total figment of imagination. Dr. Wallace is a trustworthy person and a fine scientist, and so he injected a note of doubt into my mind. In any case, the time for reflection had ended. The overland phase of the expedition was about to begin. Because Upper Dharmsala is situated in the foothills of the Indian Himalayas, it was totally inaccessible by airplane. The only reasonable way to make the long trip with all our equipment was by train and then for the remaining five hours or so by car. The train journey began fitfully, however. We were delayed eight hours in the Delhi train station because of a massive rally of more than two million farmers whom Prime Minister Indira Gandhi had called out to support her political party. The train station was teeming with people, flies, and fecal matter. In an effort to cool off and get a little bit cleaner, many of the people walked over to water pipes between the train tracks, shed their clothes, and wearing only *dhotis,* or long loincloths, took open-air showers.

When the train finally arrived, our party boarded with its twenty pieces of luggage and settled into the first-class, air-conditioned cars—an incongruous luxury, but a welcome one. Still, the trip took longer than it was supposed to, primarily because the farmers returning from the rally pulled the emergency brake cord whenever the train came close to their homes.

Finally, at two o'clock in the morning, we arrived at Amritsar, a sacred city for India's fifteen million Sikhs, which lay about forty miles from the India-Pakistan border. A dark, misty gloom hung over the train station when we arrived, and I volunteered to try to find some taxis to take us to the guest house, where we had reservations for the night. Although I found some cabs, I couldn't make the drivers understand me. The drivers were asleep on their rear seats, and many would not awaken. Dr. Malhotra, as he was to do so often, acted to resolve the problem. He found some other taxi drivers, awoke them, and we were driven to the guest house.

We arrived there at three o'clock in the morning, and after unloading the baggage, we were invited into a large wood-paneled dining room with a fifteen-foot table covered with a white tablecloth and adorned with dried sweet pastries, bread, and butter. Since there was no electricity, a young woman lit candles. As we ate in this almost reverential atmosphere, we heard Moslems being called to their prayers with piercing chants that drifted through the windows of the guest house from the outside. After a few hours' sleep, we set out by car to Dharmsala.

As we drove through India's "breadbasket," the relatively wealthy Punjab region, with the crops of mustard greens in yellow bloom, we finally sighted the snow-covered peaks of the Himalayas, which rose some twenty thousand feet into the sky. A few hours later, we arrived at Upper Dharmsala. As I mentioned earlier, the village sits on a plateau about seven thousand feet high in the mountains. From that vantage point, if you look south, you can see the plains of India stretching out below you for miles and miles. Directly beneath the city there's a sheer drop of several thousand feet to the plains below; and immediately to the north, the Himalayas rise sharply toward the heavens.

Upper Dharmsala is separated from India and the rest of the world by more than mere geography, however. It's a completely transplanted culture—a kind of Tibetan time capsule. The Tibetans have made the most of the change in location. Although there are still open sewers, they have electricity and ample food. In Tibet, the people had suffered from poor nutrition, barely grew to five feet in height, and were racked with many diseases. A person of forty was considered old. But in Upper Dharmsala, the children appeared to be quite healthy, and the teenagers, on average, were taller than their parents. In only twenty years of exile, the Dalai Lama had been able to transform his threatened culture into a thriving, industrious community.

Immediately after checking into our guest house, we met with the Dalai Lama's personal physician, Dr. Yeshi Dondon, who had offered to provide us with our meals. When we joined him at a large, rectangular dinner table, his servants brought in platters of food. Typically, they served us omelets, bread and butter, cheese, and tea for breakfast. Both lunch and dinner consisted of boiled vegetables and noodles with chopped meat and soup. The table always contained fresh fruit, usually bananas.

After we had eaten our first meal, Jeffrey Hopkins and I went to the Dalai Lama's compound to see when we could begin our experiments. But it was the Tibetan New Year, and His Holiness was too busy to meet with us—though he did send one of his representatives with a greeting.

"Is everything all set for us to study these men in their own hermitages?" I asked.

"Of course," the aide assured us. He also assured us that all of our procedures, including the use of rectal thermometers and filming, were acceptable.

We heard the Dalai Lama speak the next day to the assembled monks and other Tibetan exiles. As he walked into the courtyard under huge yellow silken umbrellas topped with long tassels, men in various feathered hats and other colorful garb sounded brass horns. We were told that in other days, the horns were made of human thigh bones. In modern Tibetan society, however, despite its firm adherence to tradition, that particular custom is no longer practiced.

The monks then began an incredible chant. Several were able to produce a chord simultaneously with two notes, an octave or more apart. One of our guides told me that this double-note sound involved a skill that took up to four years to master.

Then the Dalai Lama lectured from the Buddhist scriptures for several hours. At one point he said something softly to his followers that caused Jeffrey Hopkins to turn to me and say, "This is for you, Herb." The Dalai Lama said, "For skeptics, you must show something spectacular, because without that, they won't believe."

Afterward, the Dalai Lama's aide told us that arrangements were being made for us to begin our experiments: "We will take you there soon," he said.

Before we retired for the night, a message arrived: The way had been cleared for our work. We were to be ready at dawn to hike up the nearest mountain to the hermitage of the first monk.

4

||||||||||||||||||||||||||||||

The Phenomenon
of the
"Fierce Woman"

||||||||||||||||||||||||||||||

It comes as no surprise to most people that when they go outside on a cold day, their hands and feet become colder. Of course, the usual solution to this situation is one that's familiar to all of us—a good pair of gloves and thick socks inside insulated boots.

But a few years ago, as I have mentioned, I learned the Tibetan monks had found another way to keep their fingers and toes warm *without* clothing in even the coldest weather; and that way, I was told, was through the power of the mind. In short, they were supposed to be able to raise their skin temperature many degrees just by entering into a deep meditative state.

The monks who practice this form of meditation, *gTummo* Yoga, couldn't care less about the peripheral, practical results of their spiritual activities. For them, the heat they emanate is the by-product of a sacred religious rite. By causing their bodies to heat up through meditation, they believe they are burning false perceptions of reality out of their physical being. Literally translated, *gTum-mo* means "fierce woman"—"fierce" because the warmth is a fire of purification that decisively counteracts ingrained false ideas, and "woman" because the state is the source or "mother" that gives birth to subtler and higher states of mind.

In the past, scientists had scoffed at the monks' claims, and who could blame them? After all, the body is not supposed to get warmer when the outside temperature gets colder. In fact, the bodily reactions the monks claim are precisely the opposite of what the body normally does to maintain internal heat when it is exposed to cold temperatures. In effect, the monks seemed to be saying that the body could be "willed" to counter a basic response necessary to preserve life itself.

To explain this point more fully, let me offer a little more scientific background. Insects and cold-blooded animals such as reptiles don't function as well in the cold as they do in warm temperatures. They slow down to the point of being immobile. But mammals can thrive in a variety of climates because they can keep their internal body heat up at a relatively constant and high level. They carry within themselves a relatively constant internal temperature environment, which allows them to pursue activities in many different outside worlds. When it gets cold, mammals grow extra fur to create an additional insulating layer. In the case of humans, they put on clothing to prevent body heat from escaping.

But that's not all the body does when it gets cold. For

one thing, you can automatically begin to generate additional heat by the involuntary movements of shivering. The muscles have been called the "furnaces of the body" since their activity produces so much heat. Also, your blood vessels in the skin become constricted, and this limits the flow of blood to the fingers and toes. In this way, your body keeps its inner temperature up so that the major organs of the head, chest, and abdomen can function normally—though your extremities may get cold and even become numb or frostbitten. This is a very important process, because if the constriction of the blood vessels didn't occur, you'd quickly lose heat on a cold day. Your central or rectal temperature would begin to fall, your biochemical systems could no longer function, and you'd die.

On the other hand, the Tibetan monks were saying that they were able to retard or eliminate this constriction process just by practicing certain mental and spiritual disciplines. This was an exciting idea to me for several reasons.

First of all, I knew that scientific documentation of their claims would further support the existence of a strong basic relationship between the mind and the body. Also, such evidence would suggest that the *conscious* mind can play a much greater role in controlling the body's physical processes than many Western scientists had previously thought.

Perhaps most important of all, the ability of individuals to affect their skin temperatures at will would open up still another horizon on the mind-body frontier. If these monks could bring about significant changes in bodily functions just by following certain mental exercises, there might be other possibilities in expanding our personal power over the physical world.

Finally, in addition to the future expansion of the limits

of mind over body, there could be some very practical immediate applications of the alleged "fierce woman" phenomenon. For example, there are many people who suffer from excessive coldness in their extremities during cold weather. It was possible that these techniques could relieve this problem.

So I was eager to get on with the experiments when I awoke on the morning we were scheduled to hike to the hut of the first monk. After breakfast, the first thing on the schedule was to meet with the porters we had hired to carry our equipment up the hills. Before long, we were on the slopes, climbing a steep, rocky trail behind our guide, a Tibetan monk, who had been supplied by the Dalai Lama. The guide told us it would take several hours to reach the first hermitage by the route he had chosen. "There is a shorter way," he explained. "But it's a much rougher climb."

Because we all were feeling quite vigorous and impatient, we took a step that almost aborted our mission before it really began. Explaining that we wanted to get started as quickly as possible on the experiments, we told the guide to take us by the shorter route. He agreed, and at first, our decision seemed well taken, because the new route didn't appear to be any harder than the original path. We walked past terraces filled with brilliant, light-green mustard plants, which were in bloom. Our trek took us through the front yard of a two-story, slate-roofed farmhouse that was reminiscent of a half-timbered, sixteenth-century English Tudor building. Under the eaves was a small balcony, where a young Tibetan boy in underclothes was dressing as he watched us go by. Later we rested among rocks that surrounded a small water pool. The well-conditioned porters didn't even remove their packs but just sat and leaned against large rocks.

Then, at about nine thousand feet, the path petered out, and the hillside became much steeper. We had to climb slowly from one rock to the next, and the thinner air had us breathing heavily. When I glanced at the small Nepalese porters who were carrying our heavy equipment, however, they weren't breathing hard at all. Although they couldn't have weighed more than one hundred forty pounds each, they were easily carrying about sixty pounds of equipment each on their backs. While we had to climb with both our hands and feet, they scampered lightly up the side of the mountain. (Luckily, the weather was favorable. The temperature was fairly mild—about 60 degrees Fahrenheit—so we only needed light sweaters for warmth.)

We finally made it to a leveled portion of a ridge where we found a monk's hut—but unfortunately it wasn't the one we were looking for. As a matter of fact, it had been abandoned, and so we couldn't even ask directions.

Our guide had no idea where the monk was. It seemed that somehow after we had set off on our "shortcut," he had missed the hermitage inhabited by the monk we were scheduled to study. Apparently sensing our discomfort, the guide then tried to lift our spirits by pointing to a ridge on another slope.

"That's probably where the monk lives," he said, rather unconvincingly.

Although our confidence was shaken, we had no choice except to follow him. The second ridge wasn't too far away, but even short distances in such rough, mountainous country were an ordeal to travel. To get there meant climbing down a steep ravine and then scrambling up the other side.

It would take at least another four or five hours.

I sat down with Dr. Malhotra for a few minutes while the rest of the group climbed farther up the slope to see if they could find a more direct approach to the new ridge. Soon, they disappeared from sight, and we were left alone with our thoughts. Then, voices pierced the silence from some-place far above the spot where we were sitting: "We're O.K."

Soon, my hopeful interpretation was confirmed: The monk's hut was on this slope after all. We quickly climbed to join the others.

The hermitage was almost identical to the abandoned hut we had passed earlier. In fact, we were told, it was typical of all the huts in which the displaced Tibetan monks live. The entire place was about twenty-three feet long, thirteen feet wide, and eight feet high. It was constructed of stone but was uninsulated and unheated except for a cooking fire. There was no chimney; the smoke simply passed through the slate roof. The living quarters were small and sparsely furnished, with oil lamps, a rectangular sleeping platform, pictures of the Dalai Lama, and many Buddhist manu-scripts, which consisted of unbound rectangular sheets of paper wrapped in cloth and tied with a string. The entire scene was a reflection of the monk's ascetic life-style.

There was also a small window in the hut, and the main living area, a room about fifteen feet long and thirteen feet wide, provided barely enough room for the bed, let alone other furniture. When we entered, the first monk, "Vener-able G.J.," rose to greet us from his bed, where he had been sitting.

The conditions in which he lived were not at all unusual for this culture. Many monks spend several years in places like this with almost no contact with the outside world.

Pious supporters leave them their food weekly just outside their huts. But ordinarily, the only time they meet and talk with people is when they journey to Upper Dharmsala to participate in religious festivities or to have their meditation "checked" by a religious superior.

The Venerable G.J., who was fifty-nine years old when we met him, had been a monk since he was thirteen. He had studied in Tibet for nineteen years and then later in India for eight years. During this period, he had earned the title *Geshe,* or doctor of philosophy, and had thereby risen to one of the highest levels of scholarship. A *Geshe* must pass a rigorous oral examination that lasts many days and is administered by abbots and other prominent *Geshes.* The Dalai Lama earned his *Geshe* in Lhasa, Tibet, before he fled. In fact, he achieved the highest order of that degree.

For the past eleven years, the Venerable G.J. had continued to practice what he had learned: He had lived in near-total isolation in the foothills of the Himalayas and, along with his other religious rites, had practiced *gTum-mo* Yoga for fifteen minutes each day for the last ten years. But he said he still had not achieved the "state of bliss" that was the ultimate goal of the masters who followed this form of Yoga.

A few words about the "bliss state" may be helpful at this point. In the perfected practice of *gTum-mo* meditation, *Prana* (literally "wind" or "air") is thought to be gathered from the fragmented condition of normal human consciousness. This wind is then directed into an alleged main channel through the central part of the body, where the swirling winds ignite an intense "internal heat." The heat proceeds to "melt" a "generative" fluid that is supposed to be located in the head. Finally, as the generative fluid is drawn down and then up through the central body channel, the meditator produces succeedingly greater states of bliss.

After some brief introductions and preliminary conversation with the Venerable G.J., the time we had been waiting for so long finally arrived.

"We are here to observe your meditation," I said rather gingerly as Dr. Hopkins translated. "May we do this?"

"Normally, we do not allow this," he said. He then smiled, tilted his head, and noted quietly, "But since His Holiness says this is fine, then do as you wish."

We asked about the thermometer.

"It is fine. Do as you wish."

"May we film the proceedings?"

"Yes, of course."

It seemed we now would find out about the claims that had been made for this "fierce woman" meditation. The Dalai Lama had obviously made it possible for us to test the monks and to measure things that no scientist had ever observed before.

We unpacked our gear quickly. First of all, we attached the disk thermometers, or thermistors, to several areas of the monk's body. With these in place, we could see if his temperature varied from one part of the body to another during the experiment. Specifically, we placed them on the abdomen near the navel; on the lower back; on the chest below a nipple; on the left forearm; on the left, fifth fingernail bed (at the base of the fingernail); on the left, fifth toenail bed; and on the forehead.

We also inserted the thermometer to measure inner body temperature (the inner level of body heat remains relatively constant in healthy people). This test was especially important to enable us to determine whether any alteration in the life-sustaining body heat might accompany any changes in skin temperature.

In addition to these body-monitoring devices, we set up our portable weather station to keep track of air temperature and relative humidity. It was essential, of course, to evaluate any impact of the outside temperature on the monk's body. As it turned out, one of our later experiments could have proved invalid without this weather monitoring.

Wires from all these devices were fed into a unit that recorded each measurement. We also set up a separate unit to monitor and record G.J.'s heart rate.

We had decided to divide the experiment into three stages:

1. The "control" stage: the time before the monk actually started his meditation. During this phase we took measurements to get his normal, baseline body temperatures.
2. The "meditative" period: the time during which G.J. induced the *gTum-mo* state
3. The "recovery" period: the time when he stopped meditating and gradually emerged from the state

We took measurements every five minutes throughout all three stages. As Russell Pariseau filmed, G.J. started his meditation as he usually did, wearing only an outer robe and sitting cross-legged in the traditional lotus position. His control period was ten minutes; his meditation lasted fifty-five minutes; and his recovery ended after thirty minutes.

After the experiment got under way, we watched the changes in temperature closely. As the bodily readings started to register, there were dramatic changes. Although his inner body temperature remained stable throughout the experiment, the temperature in G.J.'s fingers increased by more than 9 degrees Fahrenheit. His toe temperature rose even more strikingly—up nearly 13 degrees Fahrenheit above the control period.

In the recovery stage, the Venerable G.J.'s finger temperature soon returned to its premeditation level, but the toe temperature stayed high for some time, perhaps because the toes were insulated against heat loss by the lotus position. The temperature increases in other areas of the monk's body were less dramatic. For example, the thermistors recorded increases of only about 2 degrees Fahrenheit on his back and near his navel.

Did the meditation alone produce these great changes in skin temperature? Our mini weather station showed that the air temperature during the experiment rose slightly, from 71.6 degrees to 74.3 degrees. But this atmospheric change by itself couldn't explain the results. In fact, the finger temperature dropped immediately after meditation—even though that was precisely the time when the air temperature was at its highest point.

As you can imagine, we were impressed. The monk exhibited a capacity to warm his skin that far exceeded any previously reported experiment in the West using biofeedback techniques. The experiment had confirmed much of what we had been told we would find. Perhaps most important of all, our findings provided strong new support for theories about the power of the mind over the body.

After the experiments had been completed, we sat for a while savoring our experience and gazing silently over the ravines, which dropped several thousand feet below us to the town of Upper Dharmsala. From that height, the houses and other buildings looked like tiny toys, and the main streets resembled minuscule lines and paths on a relief map. In the middle of the afternoon, we packed up our gear, formed our hiking line, and headed back toward town—this time on the main path, which was about nine feet wide.

That night I wondered whether the results would be repeated in our upcoming experiments on the next two monks. My mind was filled with thoughts of how often a biological experiment seems to bring positive results on only one occasion.

We were up again at daybreak, hiking toward the hut of the second monk, the Venerable J.T. He lived closer to Upper Dharmsala than the first holy man and occupied an abode in a forest of tall pine trees above Upper Dharmsala. We reached him by climbing over several landslides, but the trek was mild compared with the first. Born in western Tibet, the Venerable J.T. was forty-six years old and had entered a monastery in Lhasa, Tibet, when he was very young. Then, after studying Buddhist philosophy for seven years there, he had lived in isolation for the past eleven years in the hut where we visited him. His hut was comparable with that of G.J.

This second monk told us that he had practiced *gTum-mo* Yoga for years "without much difficulty" and that he often had achieved a state of bliss—though he doubted he had ever reached the "fully-qualified" or ultimate level of bliss. But once he started meditating, he said, the *gTum-mo* state remained with him all day long and departed only if he began to move about. He had been practicing this "fierce woman" Yoga technique four times each day and devoted about one hour to each session.

We set up the equipment and followed the basic three-stage schedule for the Venerable J.T., just as we had for G.J. J.T.'s preliminary control stage was ten minutes, his meditation went slightly longer than the first monk's— about eighty-five minutes—and his recovery lasted thirty minutes.

Once again, the results were dramatic: Although the surrounding air temperature increased during the experiment from 60 degrees to 66.5 degrees, the monk's finger and toe temperatures rose far more. His finger temperature increased by a remarkable 13 degrees, with the highest level of heat being recorded during the recovery stage. This finding confirmed what the monk had told us about his *gTum-mo* state persisting even after he stopped meditating. His toe temperature rose significantly—by about 7 degrees.

The skin temperature on other areas of the body showed more modest increases. Specifically, the skin around J.T.'s navel rose 3.4 degrees, and his chest temperature increased by about 3 degrees. As with the first monk, the Venerable J.T.'s core body temperature remained unchanged throughout the experiment.

These findings with our second monk were, as is obvious, similar to those of the first. Not only were these discoveries more startling than I had anticipated, but also they were beginning to present a consistent picture of the kind of impact that mental and spiritual disciplines could have on a particular physical response. The positive results continued on the third day of the experiments, when we visited the last monk, the Venerable L.T.

The Venerable L.T. was fifty years old, and he had been a farmer in his early years in the country north of Lhasa. He later served as a soldier in India for almost nine years, but then he renounced the military life at age forty-one and decided to become a monk.

Despite his relatively late start with religious training, L.T. had rapidly learned the material in the Buddhist religious texts through great concentration and extensive practice in meditation. For the eight years before we met him, he had lived in isolation in his hut, and he had practiced *gTum-mo* Yoga for the past six years.

Like the second monk, the Venerable L.T. said that he had successfully achieved some degree of the "bliss state," which this form of Yoga is supposed to induce. Also, once he embarked on a session of meditation, the "fierce woman" condition continued in his body all day, even in cold weather. Oddly enough, he was apparently so attuned to this form of meditation that the physical changes associated with *gTum-mo* occurred whenever he sat down, whether he was trying to meditate or not. As a result, the preliminary control measurements we took had to be done while he was still standing.

Unfortunately, our first meeting with L.T. was unsuccessful—though not through any fault of his. We performed the experiment outside his hut because it was too small to accommodate the equipment. He wore traditional Buddhist robes from the waist down and was unclothed above the waist. But the powerful sun, beating down under clear skies through a high, unpolluted atmosphere, produced a radiant-heat effect that markedly warmed his body. As a result, we were not able to tell whether it was the sun or the *gTum-mo* that produced the bodily changes.

Although I was afraid we might not get another chance to test L.T., good fortune was still with us. Because it was the Tibetan New Year, the monk was scheduled for one of his very few trips into Upper Dharmsala to listen to the Dalai Lama speak. When he came into town, we studied him again—this time in a cool hotel room in the evening, when the outside temperature was cool and there was no radiant-heat effect.

The Venerable L.T.'s session with us included a five-minute control period, a forty-minute meditation stage, and a thirty-minute recovery. As with the other monks, this meditator experienced an increase in his skin temperatures—though the rises didn't quite coincide with those of the others. For example, his finger temperature increased only 6.4 degrees, which was the lowest rise of the three; but his toe temperature rose 15 degrees—the greatest increase of all the monks. The temperatures in the other areas of his body didn't change too much, however.

As we had expected, L.T.'s internal temperature remained unchanged throughout the session. The air temperature, on the other hand, decreased from 68 degrees to 65 degrees during the meditation, and then moved up again to 66 degrees during the recovery. His finger and toe temperatures were at their highest levels when the air temperature was at its lowest.

These Tibetan Buddhists, as well as others who practice "fierce woman" meditation, are well aware that the amount of heat they produce is significant. In fact, they evaluate how far along a neophyte monk is in his practice of the Yoga by the amount of heat he can produce.

For example, they may all be asked to sit together outside on the moist, early-morning ground. The more proficient meditators can keep their skin dry with the heat they emanate, while the skin of the less able monks becomes moist from the morning dew.

In an even more striking kind of test, the monks reportedly even conduct competitions among themselves with wet, icy sheets on moonlit winter nights, similar to the practice described by Alexandra David-Neal.

For our purposes in the West, of course, the significance of *gTum-mo* Yoga lies in a somewhat different direction— that is, the medical uses of the "fierce woman" technique. If meditation of this type can cause skin blood vessels to dilate, then there may be practical ways to help people with impaired circulation. This adventure in the Himalayas has thus helped us, on one level, to define in more precise terms the power of the mind over the body. Also, the experience served as a successful test of measuring claims of supernatural powers. Although we apparently didn't find any supernatural power, we were able to observe and explain in scientific terms a phenomenon that had been considered to be supernatural.

Finally, the power of the mind over the body may well range far beyond these areas to encompass many other medical problems—problems that we have tried to treat only through physical means or, perhaps, have regarded as medically untreatable. To see how this works in practice, let's now turn our attention to how the lessons of the lamas may be applied to our own everyday health.

5

||||||||||||||||||||||||||||||

The Lessons
of the Lamas

||||||||||||||||||||||||||||||

Clearly, the meditation techniques of the Tibetan lamas, which are so deeply rooted in a Buddhist belief system, can enable them to control surface body temperatures in an unexpected fashion. But there may be some resistance to trying to learn how these Eastern practices and findings can be incorporated into our own lives.

Rationalistic, religiously skeptical Westerners may write off the "fierce woman" phenomenon as some sort of foreign or even occult trick that has no practical application to us. The condescension may turn into outright rejection when the Tibetan sages in effect tell us, "The state of your mind is the most important single factor in your physical health."

There's probably *something* to the idea of the mind influencing the body, we may concede. For example, it's certainly a good idea not to put your body under too much mental stress, or adverse physical symptoms are likely to be the result. But regarding the mind as the most important factor in our health is perhaps going too far. After all, we live in a scientific era, in the age of modern medicine.

Despite such resistance, modern medicine is beginning to recognize, even if somewhat reluctantly, that our beliefs have far more to do with good and bad health than we in the West have supposed. On the negative side, consider an epidemic that struck hundreds of Arab schoolgirls and older people in April 1983 in the Israeli-occupied West Bank region of the Middle East.

A report by the American Department of Health and Human Services noted that 943 cases of the acute illness included headaches, dizziness, sensitivity to light, blurred vision, abdominal pain, weakness, and fainting. The prevalence of these symptoms represented "an epidemic of true psychologic illness, and . . . the cause of this illness was anxiety."

The American team of investigators concluded that the spread of the illness could be traced to "psychogenic factors" that might have been "facilitated by newspaper and radio reports which described the symptoms in detail."

This is just a single, though rather dramatic example of how the mind does indeed exercise vast control over what goes on in the body. On the positive side, the long and highly developed meditational techniques in the Tibetan Buddhist culture may be responsible for beneficial effects throughout the body. We'll see just how far meditation in this and other traditions can go in helping to care for physical and emotional ills in our own culture in later chapters.

In addition to their meditational techniques, the lamas

have other lessons for us. For example, the tremendous impact that the mind can have on the body is evident in the special way the Tibetan-Buddhist physicians deal with patients. When the Tibetan doctors examine a sick person, they rely on a medical tradition that is more than a thousand years old. Their approach diverges at many points from our own approach to medical practice and in many cases highlights the key role that personal belief can play in physical healing.

In his physical examination, the Tibetan doctor may spend as much as half an hour "reading his patient's pulse." According to Tibetan medical tradition, the pulse gives more information than just indicating the speed or rhythm of a person's heartbeat. The lamas also believe it tells the doctor what's happening with the body's major organs and internal physical systems.

Unlike his Western counterparts, the Tibetan doctor gets personally involved in examining intimate things like the patient's urine specimen. He doesn't just get a technician to package it and send it to a laboratory. Instead, he conducts the inspection of the fluid himself, as he checks its color, smell, and clarity. The examining doctor will see if the urine feels oily or otherwise peculiar.

This intimate kind of involvement on the part of the doctor communicates to his patients that he cares about them as individuals. He is willing to spend time talking to them and investigates their private functions without placing some antiseptic laboratory procedure or some third party in the middle of the relationship.

When the doctor has gone through these detailed procedures, the patient is ready for a diagnosis and treatment. After identifying the person's medical needs, the Tibetan physician's next job is to make up his own medicines. He chooses from more than a thousand herbal, mineral, and animal ingredients. Some of them are quite strange and exotic—from snake meat to iron filings. Or he might pick part of a rhododendron—the lowest-growing variety—which is believed to be useful in treating jaundice and high blood pressure.

At this point, you may wonder why I seem to be dwelling on this sort of medical treatment so extensively, especially when we have not yet established, in Western terms, whether this approach is worthwhile. If a doctor in the West were to practice this kind of healing, his patients would probably reject the strange techniques and potions. In fact, he would probably lose most of his patients in short order—except for those few who were drawn to extraordinary or exotic treatments of one type or another. In extreme cases, he might even be labeled a "quack" or "witch doctor," and his professional reputation would be impaired.

People pay too much money for medical attention these days to accept the notion that their physician may be returning to the treatments of older days. So in light of our reverence for scientific medical practice, it's understandable that there would be some tendency to take the practices of the Tibetan doctors lightly. And certainly, there are very clear limits to the curative powers of the Tibetan approach. For example, it wasn't until very recently that modern antibiotics were employed by their doctors. Also, surgery was forbidden by the Tibetan Buddhist medical teachings. Furthermore, for centuries the Tibetans have relied on an assortment of "drugs" that, in themselves, may have little medical value when viewed under Western scientific scrutiny.

But strangely enough, against the expectations of our

present medical knowledge, some of these Tibetan remedies seem to do the job in bringing about medical improvements. What is the reason for their success? The only valid healing ingredient that can be identified in these cures is the presence of strong belief. The patients believed in the treatment; the doctors believed in the treatment; and the doctor and patient established a positive, trusting relationship with one another.

Of course, the importance of belief in effecting a cure would come as no surprise to those practicing medicine. In our own contemporary culture, a significant number of illnesses can be treated more successfully if the patient believes in a particular cure. This can happen even when the substance or technique the doctor uses has little or no inherent medical value. What's the secret? As with the Tibetan doctors, it's probably just the fact that the people who use the various elixirs believe they will work.

For years, Western doctors have been aware of this phenomenon of the curative power of personal belief. But they've tended to neglect any extensive study of it and instead have preferred to lump it into a catchall classification we call the placebo effect. The word *placebo* comes from a Latin root that means, literally, "I shall please." In modern medicine, it refers to a medicine or procedure that has no active, curative ingredient, but rather is given solely for the purpose of calming or pleasing the patient.

But we're learning now that our past definitions and understanding of the placebo effect are woefully inadequate. Without stopping to examine exactly why the placebo effect works or how it works, most researchers have tried to eliminate it from the repertoire of practical medicine. Studies of new drugs have been designed to minimize or completely remove the placebo effect so that the drug's "true" effec-

67

tiveness can emerge. If the effects of a new drug were not different from those of a placebo—such as a sugar pill—the new drug was considered ineffective, even though both the new drug and the placebo produced beneficial changes. In the past, little effort was expended to understand why the placebo should work at all.

Unfortunately, though, in ignoring or minimizing the power of the placebo effect, medical researchers and doctors in practice have lost one of the most powerful therapeutic forces available to man. The placebo effect can present us with some of the most dramatic examples of the power of the mind over the body and of the use of personal belief to heal a very large variety of physical maladies.

Although Western doctors may scoff at using strange herbal and mineral medicines to treat patients, we have been employing the placebo effect, often unconsciously, in another way. As we've seen, the Dalai Lama himself acknowledged that the effectiveness of Buddhist medicine depends on three things: (1) the belief of the patient; (2) the belief of the doctor; and (3) the *karma* (or spiritual force generated by their mutual actions) between the doctor and patient.

For a patient who is skeptical about the power of Buddhist religious belief, a visit to a traditional Tibetan doctor is unlikely to be very helpful. But if both the patient and the doctor start off with a belief in a common spiritual or nonphysical curative power, then remarkable things are possible. The sympathetic Tibetan doctor who asks searching questions, generally displays a good "bedside manner," and shares a common faith with his patient in Eastern healing techniques is likely to have more cures—solely because of the interaction of those three belief factors suggested by the Dalai Lama.

The best Western doctors, without using the same terminology or relying on an Eastern belief system, routinely make use of these same three factors to help their patients. Furthermore, in many cases, they do so unconsciously. Often, because our Western understanding of the placebo effect is so rudimentary, a doctor can't explain why one patient has improved or been cured and another remains ill. But in fact, we know from research into this subject that the vast majority—or about 75 percent—of the people a given doctor sees can't be helped by specific medicines or surgical techniques. Yet many people are helped merely because they visit their doctor, believe in him, and get assurances from him.

The doctor may further reinforce the patient's belief and increase the chances for a cure by letting the patient know that he's doing "all that medical science can do." However, it's not medical science but the placebo effect that is accomplishing the cure. So the doctor who gains his patient's confidence and trust is much more likely to treat an illness successfully than one who doesn't.

But let me emphasize one other important point here: In these cases I'm talking about, the doctor, by establishing a deep trust relationship with his patient, is not just treating the psychological or emotional aspects of an illness. Something quite different is involved. In short, the trust and belief interactions between doctor and patient can actually alter the patient's physiology—and effect the cure or relief of bodily diseases. Moreover, these physical changes can be measured scientifically.

Even the presence of a friend or companion who is not a doctor can make a big difference in a person's recovery. In a study of several Guatemalan mothers about to have babies, researchers probed into the effect of a "mother's companion" on the childbirth. Traditionally in Guatemala, as in many cultures, a mother is accompanied in labor and childbirth by a friend or relative who merely lends moral support.

Dr. Roberto Sosa and his colleagues have found that women who were attended by a friend during labor and birth were far less likely to have complications requiring medical intervention than were those without companions. Surprisingly, the labor of the accompanied mothers was shorter and their delivery was easier. Mothers with companions were also more likely to stay awake longer after delivery; and they smiled at, stroked, and talked to their newborn babies more.

This study suggests that a mother's companion may relieve stress and anxiety that could complicate labor and birth. In the same way, when a person visits a doctor who is reassuring, the doctor can ease mental tensions that could complicate or aggravate the individual's physical illness.

For example, when some patients about to undergo surgery were studied at the Massachusetts General Hospital, the researchers wanted to find out just how much of a difference a friendly doctor—specifically, an anesthesiologist—made in their recovery. The patients were divided into two groups by the researchers, and no one—not other doctors, hospital staff, or patients—knew to which group a given patient had been assigned. As a result, all the patients were treated routinely, without any special attention or knowledge about the study. The groups were matched according to age, sex, type and severity of their illness, and type of operation.

Before their operations, an anesthesiologist spoke to each person in the first group of patients in a rather perfunctory way. Typically, he offered a cursory explanation of the upcoming operation and briefly described the projected recovery time. This first group received no special treatment and was designated as the "control" group, with which the second group would be compared.

The second group, in contrast, received a visit from the same anesthesiologist, who devoted a few extra minutes to conversation with them. This doctor now spoke warmly with his patients and tried to establish some sort of personal bond. He listened to their concerns and worries and answered questions about the pending surgery in detail. He also told the patients what they could expect in terms of pain and discomfort during recovery. On the whole, during the five or so extra minutes this doctor took with each patient, the tone of the discussion was exceptionally upbeat, confident, and reassuring.

After surgery, clear differences emerged between the two groups. Although the hospital staff was instructed to allow as much pain-killing medication as asked for by each group, the patients in the second group—the ones who had received more personal treatment—asked for half as much as those in the first group. Moreover, the second group of patients, on average, recovered from the operations sooner than the first group, and they were discharged from the hospital on the average 2.7 days earlier.

Clearly, then, a good bedside manner does make a difference in the healing process. Or to put it another way, the human mind can significantly increase its power over the body when it is provided with a positive focus for belief. In this case, of course, the focus was a sympathetic physician who also had the authority and power to help a person back to good health.

I use the term "positive focus" here because, as we saw in the earlier illustration of psychogenic illness in Israel, beliefs can be negative as well. This dark side of the placebo effect is something we want to avoid whenever possible. There are dozens of examples throughout history of the scourge of negative placebo effects. Some even mimic terrible contagious diseases and can spread through large populations.

Here are a few illustrations:

• "Dancing manias" broke out at times in the Middle Ages, and the effects were often bizarre, to say the least. People who believed they were "possessed" jerked about wildly in the streets and danced uncontrollably. The attack might begin with signs of lassitude, tremors, vomiting, and sleeplessness. Then, the person would start leaping and dancing about for long periods of time, with tremendous amounts of endurance. The sight of one affected individual would arouse others, and sometimes groups numbering more than one hundred would fill the streets.

After hours of this frenetic, nonstop activity, the dancers would fall to the ground in a state of exhaustion. Sometimes, though, the denouement was more disastrous. According to one graphic account, some frenzied victims "dashed their brains out by running against walls and corners of buildings or rushed headlong into rapid rivers. . . ."

The cure for the attacks frequently centered on religious rites and prayer services, especially those at shrines dedicated to the patron saint of dancers and actors, St. Vitus—hence, the popular name for the manias, St. Vitus' Dance. While the notion of such an outbreak is not a worry today, the prospect was real enough in 1485 when a German town levied a fine for cursing by wishing the St. Vitus Dance upon a person.

• Epidemic convulsions broke out at a Methodist prayer meeting in England in 1812, in which an agitated church member shouted, "What shall I do to be saved?" Others in the congregation also repeated his cry, and they fell into convulsions, wild contortions, and moans of agony, according to one report.

At about the same time, similar wild expressions of religious zeal occurred in North Carolina, Tennessee, and Kentucky among a sect known as the "Jumpers." Members of this group experienced jerking about of the head, an arm, a leg, or sometimes the entire body. One person reported, "I have seen the person stand in one place and jerk backwards and forwards in quick succession, their heads nearly touching the floor behind and before. I have seen more than five hundred persons jerking at one time . . . in some very large congregations."

• Modern psychogenic epidemics often occur in close environments such as factories and schools and follow a consistent course. There is a sudden onset of nonspecific symptoms and an explosive spread of the illness, followed by a careful but unsuccessful search for the cause.

For example, during the morning shift in a Midwestern electronics plant, one worker suddenly became faint. Moments later, a colleague who had come to the aid of the first victim dropped to the floor. Within three hours, twenty workers were taken by ambulance to the hospital with complaints of headache, nausea, dizziness, and difficulty breathing. Other employees sought medical assistance from their own physicians for similar symptoms. Most of the affected individuals claimed to have noticed a strange odor in the workplace prior to feeling ill. The factory was closed while industrial hygienists searched in vain for the source of the odor and the unusual sickness. When no toxic substances were found, the plant was reopened. Within several hours, however, thirty workers reported to the medical station. Twice more the factory had to be closed and subjected to increasingly sophisticated and meticulous inspection before production returned to normal. There was a total of at least ninety-three cases of this "inhalation sickness." No environmental hazards were ever found to account for the outbreak.

• A cargo ship damaged at sea was forced to dock in New Zealand. Unlabeled containers of an unknown chemical broke open as a result of the accident and spread terrible-smelling fumes throughout the nearby town. Alarmed local officials evacuated the area, and hundreds of people were rushed to hospitals, supposedly sick from toxic inhalation. But when the chemical was finally identified, officials found that even though it may have smelled bad, it was innocuous: The substance couldn't possibly have caused a toxic reaction by itself.

• A more recent well-known example, covered extensively by the news media, was the cyanide contamination of several bottles of the aspirin substitute Tylenol. When people who used Tylenol heard that someone had poisoned bottles of the pain reliever in stores in the Chicago area, outbreaks of illness occurred in other parts of the country as well. In many instances, these illnesses seem to have resulted from the negative placebo effect and not from poisoning.

Of course, the threat of such things as toxic poisoning is very real in our contemporary society. Therefore people shouldn't be too quick to dismiss any symptoms of illness as resulting primarily from the person's state of mind. But at the same time there is a real danger of allowing anxiety to fester and spread because the physical impact of this kind of negative mental activity can be as unhealthy as actual poison. As a matter of fact, in the past twenty years there have been at least twenty-eight cases of epidemics of diseases that arose not from any physical cause but from the spread of anxiety supported by a strong belief that a real epidemic—or "poison"—was involved.

Even as we consider these examples of the negative placebo effect, remember this key point: These are not just psychological problems. They are not merely in the victim's mind or figments of his imagination. They lead to the symptoms of nausea, vomiting, diarrhea, headache, dizziness, breathing difficulty, itching, rashes, coughs, fainting, and burning of the eyes and throat. The impact of the placebo effect on the body, both for good and ill, can be very real.

In a study of a number of asthmatic patients at Downstate Medical Center in Brooklyn, for instance, researchers asked the patients to inhale an unlabeled substance, which they were told would temporarily aggravate their asthma. Sure enough, when the patients inhaled the mist, many had full-blown asthmatic attacks. They started wheezing, had difficulty breathing, and gasped uncontrollably. Yet in reality, the substance they were inhaling was a harmless saline solution.

When the patients were told they were being given an

75

antidote to the irritant, their wheezing and heavy breathing soon stopped—even though, once again, the "antidote" was the same saline solution. In other words, because these patients *believed* the investigator, their own belief systems helped bring about physiological changes.

An additional problem with the way the negative placebo effect works is that unwanted symptoms, such as wheezing for the asthmatic, often bring about more anxiety and stress. This increase in anxiety can complicate or worsen the body's responses and make recovery much more difficult.

As an illustration of this point, consider another recent study in which some patients at the University of North Carolina were about to undergo oral surgery. Researchers questioned them carefully and noted their attitudes and fears about the impending surgery. The scientists wanted to see if their state of mind had any bearing on the length of time it would take for them to recover.

In many cases, it was clear that the patients who asked the most questions about their surgery and who wanted to know every last detail about the operation fully expected a lot of pain and discomfort. They were quite anxious and apprehensive about the surgical procedure. Consequently, in a sort of self-fulfilling prophecy, these same patients often had the most problems with pain and swelling after their operations. The researchers in this study suggested that to facilitate a more problem-free recovery, doctors should pay more attention to easing their patients' anxieties *before* an operation.

But what about pills, drugs, and surgical procedures? How do they fit in with this use of the mind to heal or hurt the body?

Certainly, special drugs and surgical procedures represent a major advance in medical knowledge in the twentieth century. Indeed, these advances represent the 25 percent of illnesses with which modern Western medicine is very successful and upon which its justifiably fine reputation is based. There are infections, diseases, and other maladies that are cured every day by these scientific means. In fact, because of the power of our modern-day medicines and surgical techniques, many times the most important role that a doctor plays is that of a prescriber of pills and surgical operations. But when cures occur, it's not always clear that the pills or operations are the reason.

As an example, take the continuing debate over vitamins. For every study that promotes vitamins, another study pops up that says vitamins are worthless. Meanwhile, countless people feast daily on handfuls of vitamins because they say the pills keep them healthy and make them feel good.

I certainly wouldn't deny that these people really *do* feel better when they take their vitamins. But I suspect it's their belief in the vitamins, rather than the pills themselves, that should be given the credit. Once again, then, we return to the placebo effect—the positive, salutary side of it.

We can see the same positive power of the mind over the body with some therapeutic drugs: In certain treatments, their success is strongly linked to how well the doctor has activated his patient's faith in the drug. For example, angina pectoris, or pain in the chest associated with certain heart problems, has been treated with varying success since the disease was recognized more than two hundred years ago. But the curious thing is how much the notable success of the angina treatments remained constant with different drugs that were later proved to be of little scientific worth.

When drugs such as khellin, the xanthines, or even vitamin E were first introduced, they were widely promoted by doctors and welcomed by the public with open arms as the answer to angina pectoris. Each drug was initially successful in treating 70 percent to 90 percent of the patients who were studied by *enthusiastic* doctors. Yet whenever *skeptical* doctors studied the drug's effectiveness, the rate of success dropped to about 35 percent. Furthermore, whenever a new drug came on the market, doctors and patients alike lost confidence in the previously popular drug, and its effectiveness in treating angina plummeted.

Clearly, in these cases the drugs alone weren't responsible for the improvement in angina. What made the drugs effective was apparently the belief and positive expectations of the doctors and the patients that the drugs would work. When belief and enthusiasm diminished, so did the power of the drug.

The same placebo effect continued to work when surgical procedures were substituted for drugs in the treatment of angina. One study even went so far as actually to use a then-accepted surgical procedure—the so-called mammary-artery ligation—on one group of patients, and to *pretend* to use it by making only a useless incision under anesthesia on a second group of patients.

There are profound ethical problems with this kind of study, not the least of which is the use of deception and unnecessary surgery on the second group of patients (this investigation was performed in the 1950's—it would not be allowed today). But despite these deceitful circumstances, the study provided additional support for the power that the mind can exercise over the body. One hundred percent of the patients who did not receive the true operation reported improvement. In contrast, the condition of 76 percent of those who had the true surgery improved. In other words, the actual surgical procedure was less effective than an irrelevant skin incision.

In these examples, the doctors' enthusiasm for the new drug or procedure appears to have activated the patients' belief in the doctors and the procedures they were performing. Other studies indicate, however, that healing belief may not have to be placed in a doctor at all but rather may originate solely in the patient or his or her belief in some outside force, like God.

How many times have we heard of the recovery of a hospital patient who seemed to be beyond ordinary medical help? The doctors may step back and say, "We've done all we can—now, it's up to her." Then, contrary to all expectations, the patient somehow musters up enough inner strength, faith, or whatever to pull through a seemingly hopeless illness or injury.

In this vein, we know that as long as a patient maintains a positive outlook, his chances for survival are better than if he is negative or has resigned himself to death. In one recent medical review article, Dr. Joan Z. Borysenko of Boston's Beth Israel Hospital and the Harvard Medical School noted that researchers who have studied cancer patients have found the patients who live the longest have a number of things in common. First of all, the "long survivors" are usually "unusual individuals who do not become anxious or depressed; they are reported to have faith and inner confidence." Furthermore, they have a "fighting spirit." They *want* to be well and *plan* to be well. They say from the outset that they are going to do all they can to beat the disease.

For example, in one study Dr. E. M. Blumberg and his colleagues at the University of California, Los Angeles, investigated personality traits of male patients who were receiving radiotherapy or chemotherapy treatments for inoperable cancer. The researchers used personality traits of the patients in an effort to try to predict their survival time. The psychological characteristics were measured at a time of remission to minimize the obvious effects of advanced illness on personality. They discovered that their psychological classification could predict medical outcome in 88 percent of the patients who had a rapidly progressing disease. The most important characteristic that coincided with a rapidly progressing disease was an inability to relieve anxiety or depression.

In other important studies, researchers have found that the inability to express anger or the inappropriate expression of anger correlated with a poor outlook for the disease. In one investigation, 75 percent of the women whose initial response after a mastectomy showed a "fighting spirit" or strong denial had a favorable medical outcome five years later. In contrast, only 35 percent of those women who responded either with stoic acceptance or a helpless or hopeless outlook triumphed over their disease after five years. Initial reactions of helplessness and hopelessness occurred in 88 percent of the women who died in the five-year period. But only 46 percent of those who were disease-free at the end of the five years had expressed such negative emotions at the beginning of their illness.

In general, those "short survivors" who are least successful in fighting cancer are typically described as "despairing and helpless, in other words, as poor copers." Developing "coping skills," which foster a sense of control in most situations, has been established as important for longer survival of cancer patients in a study done by Dr. Avery Weisman and Dr. J. William Worden of Project Omega at the Harvard Medical School and Massachusetts General Hospital.

With these findings in mind, Dr. Borysenko proposed: "Behavioral interventions based on elicitation of the relaxation response provide a unique facilitation of coping" for those struggling with cancer. She also urged that investigations of this hypothesis should be performed. So we find ourselves returning once more to the meditative techniques of the Relaxation Response. In short, meditation—especially the type rooted in a deep faith of some sort—may be an excellent tool to help patients keep their spirits up, and even live longer.

As you can see from the foregoing discussions, belief—whether it's deep within your mind and "heart" or focused on some outside object like a doctor—can play a key role in generating positive or negative responses in our bodies. Beliefs that can dramatically alter the physical body may be focused on any one of a variety of different objects—a friend, a doctor, a drug, a surgical procedure, a religious being, or even a news story.

Apparently, just *having* a strong belief is enough to cause things to happen in our physiology, but this is a very ticklish point. It does seem that just the state of belief, which can emanate from a variety of personal, philosophical, or religious orientations, is itself a powerful force. Does it matter what you believe in? Belief in *something* is crucial. The very force and effectiveness of your personal belief stem from your basic assumptions that your belief matters. If you want to experience the physiological benefits of the Faith Factor and you find you have nothing to believe in, it may be helpful to believe generally in the power of the continuation of life or perhaps even just in the power of belief itself.

My intention is not to make pronouncements about the specific merits of any belief system. In this book, I'm speaking about belief only from a medical, scientific perspective and only from the vantage point of that which can be measured by the equipment and concrete tools we now have available. In this context, I can state that the placebo effect certainly has broad application for many belief systems in purely medical terms. But your individual belief system obviously goes far beyond the current, limited medical outlook presented in this book. For example, your relation to your religion or your God involves considerations other than health.

Of course, there are medical limits to what even the strongest positive beliefs can achieve for us, and so we shouldn't expect "superhealth." There simply isn't any such thing. In the first place, we all must die. So, clearly, we can't use our beliefs to create immortality or invulnerability within our bodies. In fact, in at least 25 percent of your ailments, your doctor will probably be more successful than the use of your belief system by his application of a specific medical remedy, such as a medication or surgical procedure.

But that leaves a notable *75 percent of situations where our personal beliefs can play a major role in healing physical ills.* In other words, by learning to apply the positive placebo effect as extensively as possible in our lives, we can greatly increase our level of health and personal happiness. In this regard, one of the most important ways to activate health-giving beliefs in your life is to learn to work with your physician in an intimate doctor-patient relationship. Now, let's consider some practical ways you can go about this.

PART THREE

A PRACTICAL GUIDE TO GREATER PHYSICAL AND MENTAL WELL-BEING

6

How to Work with Your Doctor Toward Optimal Health

A child who falls and cuts himself often runs to his parents for comfort and support. If the wound isn't serious, his parents won't consult with their doctor. They'll just dress the cut themselves and reassure the youngster. Sometimes, when Mom or Dad kisses the hurt arm or hand or applies a Band-Aid, the pain "magically" decreases—or at least becomes much easier to bear. Even at this early age, the power of the mind over the body is considerable.

Of course, if the wound is quite serious or if a minor wound becomes infected, it's likely that no amount of support or kissing will be enough to make it better quickly. For some illnesses you need outside help, such as a doctor.

By understanding as fully as we can the powers our minds have to help us reach our optimal health, we can reinforce our belief in the body's capacity to heal itself. The main idea is to develop a positive, powerful attitude, which provides us with a strong sense of control and equanimity, so that the best health we're capable of flows naturally from our brains to our bodies. The best combination to achieve this end seems to be a linkage between (1) a strong personal belief system, which encourages the possibility of achieving and maintaining good health; and (2) an enhancement of the healing power of this belief through the Relaxation Response. This combination is what I've called the Faith Factor.

Using this approach, we can strengthen the positive, beneficial influences our minds can have on our health, while decreasing the negative, harmful influences. When we are healthy, the Faith Factor can help us work to maintain our health. On the other hand, if we become ill, we can put our belief system to work for us, even if we're making use of drugs or surgery.

Now, here are a few guidelines to help you get the most out of your belief system as you interact with your doctor and with the techniques of modern medicine:

Step One: If you feel ill, don't hesitate to go to the doctor.

Although this may seem obvious, I am including this step to emphasize an important point: You should never play games with your health. If you feel ill, if a pain doesn't seem to go away, or if you notice any other abnormality in your body, you shouldn't make the mistake of attributing it to something like a negative placebo effect. Nor should you assume that your mind or some outside power will take care of everything without your help or that of a medical expert.

If you aren't sure of the cause of your ailment, have it checked. Try to find out from your doctor what's causing the problem. Only then will you be in a position to evaluate whether you're in the 75 percent of his or her patients who don't require specific treatment, or in the 25 percent who could be helped by a particular therapy.

Step Two: Find a supportive doctor whom you trust.

You can never overestimate the importance of warmth, concern, and a trust-inspiring style on the part of a physician. Some people may be helped simply by visiting a friendly doctor, in much the same way that a parent helps a child by kissing a bruised arm. As they reach outside for support or help, the very act of contacting a sympathetic outsider and believing that this contact will help may be enough to improve a physical problem.

But this doesn't mean that the illness or the improvement is any less real. As the study of the pregnant women in the last chapter illustrates, the mothers who were accompanied by a friendly companion during their delivery spent far less time in labor and had fewer complications during and after birth than those who lacked help. Someone offering moral support—particularly if he or she is an authority figure such as a doctor—may sometimes be the best possible medicine.

So I would strongly recommend that you be assertive and aggressive in picking the doctor who is right for you and "on your wavelength." Don't assume that every doctor is the same, either in technical skills and knowledge or in his level of personal interest in you. Shop around if the first physician you contact doesn't seem quite right, and find the one whose style and manner are consistent with and supportive of your own.

Remember: Healings are more likely to occur when the patient believes in the doctor, when the doctor believes in the patient, and when they are able to establish a harmonious relationship with one another.

Step Three: Go to a doctor who emphasizes the positive.

A doctor's upbeat attitude and belief in your ability to be cured can be infectious. If he is confident of your capacity to beat an illness, that very conviction on his part will most likely boost your own belief in yourself as well. By going to a doctor who is able to activate your belief and confidence, you'll stand a much better chance of conquering your illness.

For instance, an extreme example would be a woman who goes to her doctor for tests and finds she has cancer. Her doctor may callously say, "You have cancer. Things don't look too good. Fifty percent of those with this sort of thing die in five years."

Talk about negative thinking. If I were the patient in this situation, I would rush to get a second opinion—preferably from a doctor who would say something more like, "Yes, things aren't that good. In fact, they are quite serious. But fifty percent of people with this cancer survive at least five years. Others have successfully fought this disease, and I think you can, too."

We've all heard the old saying that a glass with water to its halfway mark is both half full and half empty. Both ways of describing that glass are true. So why not focus on the positive? Isn't it preferable to view birth as the first day of life rather than the moment one starts dying?

A positive attitude opens the vast, positive possibilities for healing. So, when you look for a doctor, pay particular attention to finding one who has a reputation for being warm, supportive, and positive. Once you find this kind of doctor, though, that's only the beginning. To get the full benefit out of a potentially powerful doctor-patient relationship, it's necessary to assert yourself at many points in the personal interaction—including the practice of prescribing medicines.

Step Four: Don't expect a prescription from your visit with a doctor.

Too often, patients who come to the end of an examination will feel they are missing something if the doctor fails to give them a prescription or place a bottle of pills in their hands. Pills have become what a patient expects in return for going to seek help.

But these days drugs are taken much too freely. The medieval physician Paracelsus said, "All drugs are poisons," and even today, that's not far from the truth. For a drug to be active, it must have side effects. There is rarely a "free lunch," even with medication. Oliver Wendell Holmes expressed a similar mistrust of medications in his time when he said, "If all the [medicines] as now used could be sunk to the bottom of the sea it would be all the better for mankind—and all the worse for the fishes."

Although medicines have improved considerably since then, the warnings still have the ring of truth. All drugs do have side effects, and we have to weigh the risk of the undesirable reactions against the drug's potential benefits. For instance, the heart medication digitalis may well be one of the most dangerous drugs in the world. Every physician who prescribes it knows that some of the people who take the drug become quite ill from its side effects. Yet we prescribe it because it's far more likely that many more patients who need it will markedly benefit from it than will be harmed.

The key point here, though, is that you don't always have to get a pill to get well. The visit to the doctor in itself may be sufficient to engage your inner belief systems and speed you on the way to recovery. So begin to learn to rely more on your mind than on medicine. And don't request a prescription if the doctor doesn't offer one.

Step Five: If drugs or surgery are prescribed, find out why.

If your doctor prescribes a drug that you know is a recognized effective treatment for your illness, there's every reason to accept the prescription readily. But if you ascertain that the pills you receive act only through the placebo effect, this means you're probably among the 75 percent of all patients who don't necessarily have to be helped by direct, specific treatments like a drug. After all, 35 to 45 percent of all prescriptions are essentially placebos. Furthermore, in 1979 investigators found that there were more than six hundred drugs on the market in the United States that were no more effective than a placebo. One in eight prescriptions filled by pharmacists—or 169 million prescriptions worth $1.1 billion—were for drugs considered ineffective by the federal government.

When a physician prescribes an antibiotic for a bacterial infection, he knows that the medicine has been proved effective against a particular type of infection you have. On the other hand, if your doctor writes a prescription that is designed to ease the discomfort of, say, mild joint pains or a tension headache, then he may be responding to pressure to fulfill your expectations for visiting his office.

Doctors are only human and will respond to your needs. They've been trained to believe that they should try to do something when a patient comes to see them. As a result, they may write a prescription, even when the need for the medicine is marginal at best and even though many would prefer not to give any treatment.

The pressure on doctors to prescribe drugs has become widespread. For example, take the problem of hypertension. In a recent report to Congress, the assistant secretary for health said that lifelong drug treatment effectively prolongs life in people with mild or borderline hypertension. That's enough to give many physicians confidence in prescribing drugs for this ailment—but the possibilities are staggering. You see, the number of people with this kind of mild hypertension amounts to about one fifth of the adult population of the United States. With this many people taking a drug, it's essential to be absolutely sure that the benefits outweigh the risks.

What bothers me about the "prescribe in most cases" approach is that drugs that combat mild hypertension, like most other drugs, often have toxic effects. Or, more commonly, they may disturb the drug user's quality of life, including his ability to function energetically with regard to his daily demands. Also, the male sexual function is frequently impaired.

So is it really a good idea to put people on a lifelong drug program to treat mild hypertension when the risks of this disease, though real, may be less than the risks of the drugs?

Some researchers and government officials are answering "yes" to this question. If drug treatment is effective, they say, it's worth the increase in risk to some people in order to improve the ultimate health of the great majority. Yet others are now advocating nondrug treatments of mild hypertension. These treatments, which have virtually no serious side effects and can effectively lower blood pressure, include elicitation of the Relaxation Response; reduction of the amount of table salt eaten; weight loss; and exercise. Very often blood pressure is lowered by the use of such a program, and drugs are not necessary.

Patients who are offered prescription drugs by their doctors should ask some questions to find out if they really need the treatment. In other words, you should probe gently and diplomatically to learn if the pills you're getting are intended to treat the illness or merely treat your worries about the symptoms.

It's also a good idea to explain to your doctor why you're asking these questions, thus giving him an opportunity to open better lines of communication with you. In this regard, you might take some clues from your doctor. Suppose you come in with a pain in your head, and he says, "Oh, it's a common type of headache, nothing really to worry about. It'll go away soon. But take two of these, three times a day for a week, and you'll feel better."

That sort of introduction to medication should raise red flags in your mind. Stop him at this point and ask, "Do I really need this medicine? Are there nondrug approaches I might use?"

If he insists you need the medication, you might then ask, "Might I get along with less of it each time I take it? Or how about taking it for a shorter period of time?"

If the doctor agrees to any of your suggestions, then you can assume that the drug does not provide a curative treatment for your specific ailment. Instead, it's one that may be acting to relieve your worries about the symptoms.

But even though the drug is not specifically curative and

is directed toward the symptoms rather than the source of the disease, you may still want to use it as a sort of "bridge" to get the curative forces of the Faith Factor operating in your life. Here's the way this might work: In the course of an examining-room conversation, the doctor has indicated that the pills are not essential to your recovery. But at the same time, he has assured you that you *will* recover, and you can do so completely on your own, in the natural course of events.

In this case, you might ask your doctor, "Can I see whether or not I can get well without taking the pills at all? I'd still like the prescription, to keep in my pocket just in case. But will it be okay for me to take a dose only if I feel I need it?" If your physician goes along with this idea, you'll have embarked on an important new phase of testing the power of your belief in your capacity to be healed.

Still, there are some physicians who don't feel that sitting and listening to people and reassuring them is doing enough. They've been trained in the scientific discipline of analyzing a medical problem and then zeroing in on the possible source of the problem and the probable cure. Treatments, according to this way of thinking, must involve doing something specific to the body. That is, whenever possible, you should act directly to change the body chemistry or remove the offending part. In this view, talking or holding a patient's hand isn't really doing anything; it's either a cop-out or a stopgap until you can find out the real answer to the patient's problem.

Other doctors arrange their office hours and their interactions with patients in accordance with this pressure to come up with a specific, outside physical solution to a physical problem. Little or no premium is placed on the bedside manner as an important factor in the healing process. In fact, spending too much time with a patient can work against the doctor's ability to build up a practice because more time per patient means fewer patients and hence, a smaller total income. A doctor is often paid the same for an office visit, regardless of whether it takes him ten minutes or forty-five minutes to deal with the patient. As a result, it behooves him to spend as little time as possible with each patient and to encourage a rapid turnover of office visits each day. Furthermore, doctors are paid more depending on the number of procedures they perform, such as laboratory tests.

But even though extra tests may hike your bill, they may not be very effective in healing you or even identifying your problem. So it's important to ask your physician at every step along the way whether or not a given laboratory procedure is really necessary for the ailment you've asked him to examine.

One way to be polite about this, without giving the doctor the impression you mistrust him, is to ask, "Can you explain to me what this test is supposed to show? If it is not absolutely necessary, could we do without it?"

If your doctor is vague or can't (or won't) provide you with meaningful responses, then it is wise to seek a second opinion. Also, beware of physicians who insist on many tests *before* you are interviewed. After all, how does the physician know what tests you need if no questions have been asked?

Let me offer one word of caution at this point: It's important not to alienate your doctor by seeming to accuse him of performing tests of little value. The chances are he has a good reason for what he is doing. If you seem to mistrust him, the all-important relationship between the two of you will probably be damaged. Moreover, the healthful effects of the Faith Factor, which is based in part on the doctor-patient relationship, will be undermined. So it's important to be careful and diplomatic, even as you become more assertive in your interactions with your physician.

Today surgery is offered for some of the diseases in the 75 percent category in which a mind-body interaction can be of major beneficial import. The risks of such unnecessary surgery have been well publicized and have resulted in campaigns to teach patients to ask for a second opinion. In one recent study, researchers found that illness caused by surgery itself occurred once every ten days in a 332-bed hospital. Not only that but these surgical mistakes resulted in the death of the patient 55 percent of the time. There are several factors that have led to this abuse of surgical procedures:

1. Doctors are too quick to choose the surgical option when it really isn't necessary.
2. Overoptimistic doctors sometimes ignore or misread signs of complications that may follow surgery. As a result, the patient develops a physical problem that could have been caught and adequately treated with a little more attention during the early postoperative phase of treatment.
3. Surgeons often use what is known as "vogue therapy," or surgical procedures that are in vogue or fashionable at the moment. These procedures may have been developed quite recently, and glamour or prestige may be attached to using them. In other words, there's the tendency to "go for the headlines" in surgery as well as in many other pursuits in life.

95

So I would urge all patients who are told by their doctors that they need surgery to go to an independent physician for his opinion. It's also helpful to get a second opinion from a nonsurgeon and to explore other nonsurgical options for treatment. No surgery may be necessary, and a safe and effective treatment program may evolve.

This fifth step, which involves your evaluation and your physician's of the need for drugs or surgery, is extremely important in achieving good health, because the biggest hurdle a person must clear is often the mistaken belief that he always needs these treatments to get well. As you put prescribed medicine in its proper place, a next step, the use of the Relaxation Response, should also become a key ingredient in your personal health program. Often, you'll find the Relaxation Response works as well as or better than drugs. Even if your doctor insists that you use the drug or undergo the surgery he has prescribed, you'll find this final step can serve as an important adjunct to your treatment.

Step Six: Use the Relaxation Response regularly.

The elicitation of the Relaxation Response is a treatment that will be described in detail in the following chapters, but the basic procedure goes like this:

• Sit in a comfortable position.
• Close your eyes and relax your muscles.
• Focus on your breathing. Breathe slowly and naturally.
• Select a word, prayer, or phrase, such as the number "one" (or, even better, a word or phrase that is rooted in your belief system—but more on this later). Then, repeat it silently or see it in your mind's eye each time you exhale.

• When outside thoughts intrude during the meditation, disregard them by saying, "Oh, well," and return to the word or prayer you've selected. It's essential always to maintain a passive, relaxed style in dealing with any interruptions.

I have mentioned the importance of eliciting the Relaxation Response as one of the two necessary components of the Faith Factor. The other, of course, is belief. The two build upon each other. When we are stressed, worried, or too concerned about our health, or when a symptom of an illness plagues us, we experience anxiety. The anxiety then becomes an essential feature of a self-perpetuating "anxiety cycle."

In other words, if we begin by feeling some anxiety about something, this activates the sympathetic nervous system— the portion of the nervous system that becomes more active during emergencies or stress. The sympathetic nervous system, in turn, aggravates and worsens the effects of the stress, including the emotional and physical symptoms of illness. This worsening of symptoms feeds back into the initial feelings of anxiety. Then, the cycle begins again, with an even greater negative impact on our minds and bodies.

You see, anxiety causes a "turning-on" of the sympathetic nervous system through a mind-body connection. This activation of the nervous system makes the stress, worry, or physical symptoms worse, and the entire process escalates, causing more anxiety. The effects of the sympathetic nervous system are brought about through the action of the hormones adrenaline and noradrenaline, or epinephrine and norepinephrine. An overabundance of these substances has been related to the development of a number of illnesses: anxiety, hypertension, cardiac rhythm dis-

THE ANXIETY CYCLE

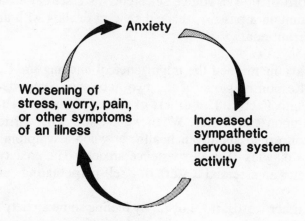

Anxiety

Worsening of
stress, worry, pain,
or other symptoms
of an illness

Increased
sympathetic
nervous system
activity

turbances, backaches, tension headaches, insomnia, and
muscle aches.

An example of what happens to your sympathetic nervous system can be seen when you slam on the brakes in your car. Impulses from your brain cause the nerves of the sympathetic nervous system to release adrenaline or noradrenaline, which produces an increased heart rate, higher blood pressure, a faster respiratory rate, more blood flowing to the arm and leg muscles, and a higher metabolism.

In an emergency, the action of these substances stimulates your system to prepare you for "fight or flight." These hormones were especially important in helping our ancient ancestors meet the challenges of more primitive times when human beings were hunters facing regular danger from wild beasts and predators. Acting as stimulants, they put the human's nerves and muscles "on edge" so that he was ready to repel an aggressor or run away from him. But in our own day, emotional stresses have replaced physical ones. As a result, we can't usually take the physical actions necessary to dissipate the stimulation of these hormones, and so these powerful substances tend to "attack" the body instead of enabling it to deal better with outside forces.

To treat medical problems caused by the body's stress-producing substances, a doctor may prescribe a so-called beta-blocking drug, which partly blocks the effects of these hormones. But there's another way to achieve similar results—the Relaxation Response. Studies have shown that this Response doesn't decrease the amount of norepinephrine released by the nerves. But it does tend to change the response to the hormone so that the hormone has less of an effect.

Therefore, the Relaxation Response breaks the vicious cycle by blocking the action of the hormones of the sympathetic nervous system. This blockage prevents anxiety and other harmful effects.

Furthermore, the bringing forth of the Relaxation Response tends to break up some of the inappropriate "loops" of thinking formed in the "wiring" of your brain (see Chapter Two). The focusing of your thinking on a word, sound, prayer, or exercise breaks the chain of everyday worrisome thought.

The Relaxation Response can be helpful in at least two ways as you deal with your health problem. First of all, if your physician is treating you with drugs or procedures that are intended to relieve the worries about symptoms rather than treat the cause of your ailment, the Relaxation Response may be all the therapy you need. Second, even if you are suffering from something that requires specific

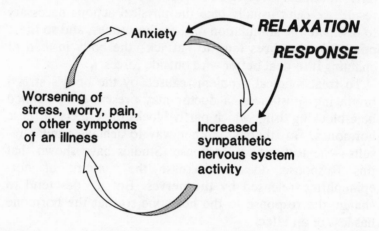

treatment, such as a drug or surgery, your cure may be hastened if you use the Relaxation Response in conjunction with other specific therapies.

When the Relaxation Response is used correctly, it may also enhance your belief in your ability to be healed, and an effective treatment may result. The Tibetan Buddhists, among others, believe that meditation causes a positive disturbance in the universe and that it puts them in tune with the universe's beneficial energies. When they use meditation to heal, they believe they tap into these healing energies. The ancient Egyptians called these powerful forces *Ka,* the traditional Chinese called them *Chi,* the Indians refer to this power as *Prana,* and the Hawaiians use the term *Mana.*

In each of these cultures, healers or "doctors" act as a conduit for the healing forces by meditating themselves and directing this energy into the person to be healed. These folk physicians are considered to be a sort of lightning rod for the universal healing forces. Whatever theological or philosophical reasons may be given for the power of meditation in these cultures, the techniques all commonly elicit what we today call the Relaxation Response.

What makes the Relaxation Response a particularly effective tool is that it can join forces with the beneficial power of your belief system. You can use a Relaxation-Response technique to enhance your health either by combining it with a belief in a power outside of yourself, such as a religious being, or you can employ it along with your belief in your body's ability to heal itself.

In the next chapter, I'll show you how this Faith Factor works—how you can practice the Relaxation Response in a manner that's tailor-made to your own belief system. In this way, the combined forces of your personal, positive beliefs and the proven benefits of the Relaxation Response can work with modern medicine to help you reach your optimal level of physical health.

7

The Fundamentals of the Faith Factor: How to Combine the Relaxation Response with Your Personal Beliefs

It may not even be daylight when your alarm jars you from your sleep. Still blurry-eyed, you make your way to the bathroom and try your best to start waking up. Before you know it, your mind is already in high gear—anticipating the day ahead, planning work, organizing activities, setting priorities.

As you remember tasks left undone yesterday or nagging problems that you'll have to face again today, tension begins to mount—and may well continue to increase throughout the day. What's happening here is the reawakening of what I have called the "anxiety cycle." Your anxiety cycle may be related to a difficult situation at work, a relationship at home, an illness in your family, concerns about your own health and limitations, or, indeed, about death itself. The process feeds on itself, intensifies, and often leads to various health problems. For example, this kind of inner tension can result in headaches, insomnia, or even, after a period of time, hypertension and heart disease.

Everyone has experienced this kind of anxiety cycle at one time or another, and certain people manage the problem better than others. But at some point, almost everyone could use a little extra help, such as a technique that will act as an antidote.

Sometimes, the helpful technique may involve nothing more than standing up from your desk and walking around a few paces if you happen to be mentally stuck or blocked by your anxiety cycle on a particular report you're writing. Or it may be a matter of taking a coffee break or otherwise interrupting the thought-chain that has you imprisoned. A vacation may be necessary.

But many times these informal approaches aren't enough. They may work, but their impact often isn't comprehensive or broad enough to cover the wide range of worries and tensions that you encounter each day and that "feed" your cycle. It's at this point that the Relaxation Response is useful. This phenomenon can be elicited through relatively simple forms of meditation or prayer, which allow your mind to "settle down" and move into more productive thought patterns. By providing an escape hatch for your conscious mind, then, the Relaxation Response creates an oasis of calm from the many thoughts and pressures that clamor for your attention each day. In this way, you can develop a consistently effective tool that will counter tension and its accompanying ills by breaking the vicious cycle of anxiety.

If you find this somewhat hard to follow in the abstract,

let me introduce you to this use of the Relaxation Response in more concrete terms. Just close your eyes for a few moments and notice the various thoughts that enter your mind. One second you may be on one train of thought, such as a racing daydream, and the next second another idea or concern may interrupt and totally redirect your thinking.

The way the Relaxation-Response technique gives your mind a rest from these mental onslaughts or loops of thinking is by the special use of a verbal device, such as a sound, word, prayer, or phrase. Specifically, you silently repeat the phrase over and over to yourself as a calming focus for your attention and as a means of breaking the chain of everyday thought.

The Relaxation-Response technique you use usually won't have any dramatic, immediate effect, even though you may feel more rested and refreshed after the first session. The long-term physical and emotional benefits, on the other hand, will become quite evident after you've practiced the technique regularly, over an extended period of weeks. Furthermore, as you already know, we are discovering that the potential for this simple Relaxation-Response technique increases when it is exercised in the context of a person's belief system. In such a case, the inner capacity to combat tension, treat physical problems, and otherwise increase mental powers in one's life accelerates. In other words, the Relaxation Response can be used to bring about the Faith Factor, as personal belief enhances those tension-fighting inner powers. These benefits will multiply as you rely on the Faith Factor—or the combination of a Relaxation-Response technique with your deeply felt personal system of belief.

Herbert Benson, M.D.

Now, in practical terms, here are the steps you should take to introduce the Faith Factor into your life:

Step One: Pick a brief phrase or word that reflects your basic belief system.

To get the maximum benefit out of the Relaxation Response, you should tailor it to your personal belief system. Since a most crucial part of any Relaxation-Response technique is to use a word or phrase to focus or meditate on, it's important to pick a word that has a special meaning to you. In that way, the focus phrase you use will reinforce the basic power of the Relaxation Response by allowing the Faith Factor to have its effects. The Relaxation Response will work whether you believe in it or not if you follow the basic instructions that bring it forth. The healthful effects of decreased sympathetic nervous system activity will still occur. But it's similar to receiving the same effective treatment from two physicians. If you trust and believe in only one of the physicians, the treatment will be *more* effective in his hands.

By using a word or phrase with an important personal meaning, you'll activate your beliefs in a way that will also encourage a healthful placebo effect. For example, as we'll see later, the Relaxation Response brings about relief from anxiety and is an effective treatment for a number of diseases. The more your beliefs are integrated into the Relaxation Response, the greater your chances of making use of the Faith Factor.

Furthermore, if you regularly focus your attention on a word or phrase that is tied into your basic personal beliefs, it's more likely that you'll get more deeply involved in the Relaxation-Response technique. You'll look forward to practicing it, and you'll do it more consistently.

So choosing a personally important word or phrase to focus upon can serve a dual function: (1) It can activate your belief systems and the accompanying benefits by providing a greater calming effect on your mind than you might achieve with a neutral focus word; and (2) it increases the likelihood of your use of the technique.

What word or phrase should you choose?

There are countless answers to this question. The only limitation I would suggest is that the words or phrase should be short enough to be said silently as you *exhale* normally. Generally speaking, this means that six or seven words would be the maximum number you should consider for your focus words.

Hindu or other Eastern religious traditions that practice meditation have certain words or mantras. But many Westerners, and especially those committed to a form of Christianity or Judaism, are reluctant to use these terms. In fact, the use of the mantra, which may include the names of Hindu gods, may actually have a negative effect and cause more unrest and anxiety than peace of mind if you don't believe in them. It's important for those from every religious and philosophical tradition to understand that there are alternatives that can fit into their own set of convictions.

Here are some examples of alternative focus words that are used with Western religions.

Roman Catholics and Christians from related traditions may use:

- A variation on the well-known Jesus prayer: "Lord Jesus Christ, have mercy on me"
- A line from the Our Father, or the Lord's Prayer: "Our Father, who art in heaven," or "hallowed be Thy name," or some similarly short phrase

- A line from the Hail Mary: "Hail Mary, full of grace"
- A line from the Apostles' Creed: "I believe in the Holy Spirit"
- A phrase from Mary's Magnificat, Luke 1:46-55: "My soul magnifies the Lord"
- A line from Zechariah's Benedictus (Blessed) in Luke 1:68-79: "Blessed be the Lord God of Israel"
- The opening words of the Prayer to the Holy Spirit: "Come, Holy Spirit"
- The final words from the Prayer for the Pope: "Unity in faith and love"

Protestants may use the phrases above that seem appropriate to their personal beliefs, or any of the following:

- Words from Psalm 23: "The Lord is my shepherd"
- Words from Psalm 100: "Make a joyful noise unto the Lord"
- Any of Jesus' teachings or words, such as: "My peace I give unto you" (John 14:27), or "Love one another" (John 15:12), or "I am the way, the truth, and the life" (John 14:6)
- Any other meaningful passage from the New Testament, such as: "The peace . . . which passes . . . understanding" (Phil. 4:7), or "We have the mind of Christ" (1 Cor. 2:16)

Jewish people of any tradition (and many Christians, as well) should be comfortable with focus words and phrases like these:

- The Hebrew word for peace: *Shalom*
- The Hebrew word for "one": *Echod*

- Any passage from the Old Testament, such as "You shall love your neighbor" (Lev. 19:18), or "God said, 'Let there be light'" (Gen. 1:3)
- Focus phrases that conform to King David's practice of meditating on God's promises, precepts, law, works, deeds, wonders, name, and decrees. (For a sampling of David's choice of subjects for meditation, see Psalms 76:11-12; 104:34; 111:2; 119:15, 23, 27, 48, 55, 97, 105, 148.) For example, you might pick Psalm 119:105: "Thy word is a lamp unto my feet."
- Lines from Jewish worship and devotional literature, such as these, taken from the *Daily Prayers with English Translation* by Dr. A. Th. Philips: "O God . . . Thy loving kindness," "No unity like unto His," "He hath remembered His covenant for ever," "The Rock of our lives," or "The Shield of our salvation"

This same sort of approach to selecting appropriate focus words and meditative phrases and prayers can be applied in any other belief system or philosophical world view. For example, Moslems might want to repeat words like the following:

- The word for God, *Allah*
- Some of the words said to be uttered to Mohammed by Allah at the Prophet's initial call: "Thy Lord is wondrous kind . . ."
- The words of the first Moslem who called the "faithful" to prayer. Though his master tortured him by depriving him of water in the desert, he kept repeating *ahadum*, or "One [God]" until his master relented.

Herbert Benson, M.D.

And those from the Hindu and Buddhist traditions will find a wealth of phrases that are currently used in the special meditative techniques of those faiths. For example:

- The Bhagavad-Gita, the Hindu Scriptures, says, "Joy is inward."
- Mahatma Gandhi said, "Turn the spotlight inward."
- Part of a favorite invocation of Hindu priests: "Thou are everywhere" and "Thou are without form"
- Buddhist literature contains phrases like these: "Life is a journey" and "I surrender indifferently."

Of course, if you don't happen to affirm a traditional religious faith, the Faith Factor can still be an important, healing part of your life. In fact, the research has shown that *any* neutral sound or word can be effective in eliciting the Relaxation Response. So even if you deny that religious or broad philosophical convictions are valid at all, you can get significant benefits from the Faith Factor. Simply pick a word like "one," which I described in my initial instructions for eliciting the Relaxation Response. Strongly affirming the presence and power of the Relaxation Response itself may be sufficient to trigger the Faith Factor.

But now, let me mention a few considerations related to this procedure of picking an appropriate word or phrase. First of all, whatever word or group of words you choose should be easy to pronounce and remember. Second, as I've already mentioned, the words should be short enough to say silently as you exhale a breath.

Finally, it's important to remember a basic point I'm trying to make in this book: An ability to combine the Relaxation Response with your personal belief system can produce the powerful inner effects of what I've called the

Faith Factor. As a result, achieving this link between belief and the Relaxation Response can make a difference in the final effect.

But even as I make these statements, I'm not trying to promote one religious faith over another, nor indeed am I advocating religion. I am saying that it does make a difference what you believe because your conviction about the unique power of your faith—at least for yourself—plays a central role in what you can achieve with the Faith Factor.

What I am also saying is that the Faith Factor involves *techniques* that are not limited to any one religious or philosophical system. In other words, the same basic approach—which has a quantifiable, scientifically measurable effect—can be applied in a variety of specific circumstances and faith contexts. Furthermore, in all these contexts, there seems to be a similar potential for health-enhancing effects, even though the substantive content of the focus words or prayers is different.

Most religions stress the importance of an inspired literature from God—though the specifics of those writings may be as different as the Bible, the Koran, and the Lotus Sutra. No one would deny that religious writings are one of the cornerstones of all these traditions, and that an allegiance to the teachings in these writings has been a central moving force in each faith. Yet, each set of writings is quite different and distinct from all the others.

Similarly, most of the major faiths and many philosophical systems as well have at one time or another found great benefits from meditative and other practices that elicit the Relaxation Response. Their techniques and the health-giving results are similar, even though the content of the meditation—including the focus words—is different.

Therefore, your belief system definitely does make a difference in how you, personally, can make the best use of the Faith Factor. But the operation of the Faith Factor is not limited to any one set of religious or philosophical convictions.

But now, having said that, let me move on to the next steps that show how the words and phrases you've chosen should be used in the practical context of the Relaxation Response.

Step Two: Choose a comfortable position.

When people meditate in many cultures, they sit in a "lotus" position, with their legs crossed and their hands on their knees. Sometimes, people stand and sway back and forth slowly as they pray, as with the *davening* practice of Orthodox Jews. But the Relaxation Response can be brought forth just as well when you sit in any comfortable position that won't disturb your thoughts.

The variety of positions developed in other cultures may be no more than a ritualistic way of keeping the meditating person from falling asleep. For example, many Protestants may kneel. The founder of Methodism, John Wesley, set aside a special little alcove in his parsonage in London, with a kneeling stool, so that he could pray in this preferred position. Certain Catholics and Buddhists, on the other hand, may prostrate themselves stomach-down on the floor, with their faces to the ground. These positions are comfortable enough so that they can be maintained for relatively long periods, but they are uncomfortable enough so that the practitioner won't doze off.

An early example of the problem of sleepiness during prayer may be the experience of Jesus' disciples, who fell asleep more than once in the Garden of Gethsemane while their Master was praying nearby. Jesus chided them for that and urged them in no uncertain terms to "watch and pray." The *Catholic Encyclopedia* puts emphasis on attentiveness during all forms of prayer: "Attention is the very essence of prayer; as soon as this attention ceases, prayer ceases."

In some cases, if you're suffering from insomnia, you'll want to use the Relaxation-Response technique to help you fall asleep, and we'll provide some detail on this technique in the next chapter. In most cases, your Relaxation-Response method should not put you to sleep. The technique is restful, however, and so while you should make yourself comfortable, you don't want to lie down or sit in such a way that you could easily drift off to sleep.

Step Three: Close your eyes.

Avoid squinting or squeezing your eyes. Close them easily and naturally. The act should be effortless.

Step Four: Relax your muscles.

Starting with your feet and progressing up to your calves, thighs, and abdomen, relax the various muscle groups in your body.

Loosen up your head, neck, and shoulders by gently rolling your head around and shrugging your shoulders slightly. As for your arms and hands, stretch and then relax them, and then let them drape naturally into your lap. Avoid grasping your knees or legs or holding your hands tightly together.

Step Five: Become aware of your breathing, and start using your faith-rooted focus word.

Breathe slowly and naturally, without forcing your rhythm. At this point, start repeating silently the word or phrase you have chosen as your mental device on each out-breath.

For example, if you use the word *Shalom,* slowly breathe in and then out. As your breath is going out, say *Shalom* silently to yourself. If you have chosen an entire phrase, such as "The Lord is my shepherd," silently repeat the entire phrase as you exhale. In other words, breathe in silently, and then while breathing out, repeat silently that line from Psalm 23.

If you have not been able to find any word or phrase that conforms to your beliefs, you can elicit the Relaxation Response without saying any words to yourself at all. Instead, as you breathe in, focus your awareness on the expansion of your abdomen, and then on its contraction as you exhale. Visualize your abdomen as if it were a balloon that slowly fills and then slowly empties—filling and emptying, filling and emptying.

Remember, though, the more you tailor the relaxation technique to your own beliefs, the more likely it is that you'll continue to use it regularly and get the full benefits of the Faith Factor.

Step Six: Maintain a passive attitude.

Along with the repeated word, sound, phrase, prayer, or thought, a passive attitude is the other most crucial aspect of eliciting the Relaxation Response. As you sit quietly, repeating your personal phrase or prayer silently, thoughts will inevitably begin to bombard your mind. You may even see mental images or patterns that distract you from your chosen word or phrase.

But remember: They don't matter. These lapses are natural and they happen to everyone who practices a Relaxation-Response technique. The key to dealing with these interruptions is learning to respond to them in a casual, unconcerned way. Do not try to force or concentrate them out of your mind.

If a distracting thought or image comes into your mind, or if a siren or some other noise momentarily grabs your attention, or if a pain of an ailment you have becomes bothersome, simply adopt a passive attitude. In other words, don't fight the distraction. When you become aware of it, simply say to yourself, "Oh, well," and slip gently back into the repetition of your phrase. An aggressive attitude toward intrusive thoughts is precisely what you should avoid. Even if these thoughts or sounds persist throughout the entire time you are meditating, that's all right. They are natural. Even though there are other thoughts during virtually every moment of meditation, I have found that if you maintain a passive attitude and return to your repetition as you recognize the other thoughts, the physiologic changes of the Relaxation Response will occur.

In the same way, if you're distracted by an itch or tight clothing, go ahead and scratch or rearrange your clothes so that you're more comfortable as you continue with your chosen focus words. Through regular practice, you can learn to disregard the aggressive, unsettling thoughts that push their way into your consciousness—including even the bothersome thoughts about how well you are practicing the technique and whether it is working.

Your attitude toward practicing a Relaxation-Response technique should be almost as matter-of-fact as brushing your teeth in the morning. Brushing, after all, is part of your usual daily routine and becomes an automatic process that you probably don't think much about while you're performing it. Most likely, you don't expend too much time thinking about whether or not you're achieving your ultimate goal of preventing cavities and eliminating bad breath. You don't worry afterwards, "That was really a bad job of brushing. I'll have to do better this evening." Nor do you think, "That was a marvelous brushing experience!" Rather, you execute this task in a routine way, and you expect that somewhere, down the line, you'll reap certain benefits because you're doing what's most helpful to prevent tooth decay.

Step Seven: Continue for a set period of time.

Practice the technique for only ten to twenty minutes. But don't time your session with a kitchen timer, alarm watch, or other kind of alarm. This would startle or jolt you—or make you anticipate the sound—and that kind of influence would work against the necessary passive attitude.

Instead, keep a watch or a clock in plain sight, and sneak a peek now and then when you think about the time. If the ten to twenty minutes have not passed, close your eyes again and return to the repetition until the full time has elapsed.

Once your session is over, sit quietly but keep your eyes closed for a full minute or two. Stop repeating the word or phrase you've been using. Allow regular thoughts to enter your consciousness once again. Finally, open your eyes slowly, and sit quietly for another full minute or two. If you stand up immediately, you may feel slightly dizzy. The dizziness is not dangerous, but there is no need to experience it. As you elicit the Relaxation Response by slowly going into it, so should you return to your everyday state in a slow, gradual manner.

Step Eight: Practice the technique twice daily.

You should use the method twice a day. Most people do so before breakfast and before dinner. The exact time that you schedule your sessions is up to you, but the method seems to work best on an empty stomach.

One reason for this is that during the elicitation of the Relaxation Response the flow of blood is directed to the skin and muscles of the arms and legs and perhaps to the brain, and away from the abdominal area. As a result, its effects may compete with the digestion process. So, by using the technique just after a meal, you may not achieve maximal results. A good time to use the method is before eating or several hours after a meal. It's interesting to note how many meditative prayers over the centuries have been taught to be utilized with some form of fasting.

In these steps, then, you have the basic procedure you need to combine the Relaxation Response with your personal belief system—a combination that can introduce the powerful, relaxing, healing Faith Factor into your life. There are a number of other uses and variations of these basic steps, including ways to treat health problems and also to bring forth the Relaxation Response during exercise. I would like to turn our attention to those approaches now.

8

||||||||||||||||||||||||||||

The Way to
Power over Physical
and Mental Problems

||||||||||||||||||||||||||||

The Faith Factor, which combines the Relaxation Response with your personal belief system, will not be a panacea for every ill you face in your life. But properly employed, it can accomplish remarkably effective results through direct chemical actions in your body.

For example, the Faith Factor can:

- Break the anxiety cycle and relieve the anxiety-related symptoms of nausea, vomiting, diarrhea, constipation, and short-temperedness
- Combat attacks of hyperventilation
- Alleviate the pains of headache, backache, and other pains, such as angina pectoris

- Effectively treat many types of hypertension and heart-beat irregularities
- Alleviate insomnia
- Be utilized in the treatment of cancer
- Prevent the harmful effects of stress
- Be employed during exercise
- Enhance creativity

These might seem like excessively far-reaching claims for a relatively simple Relaxation-Response technique coupled with belief, but there is now much supportive scientific evidence. Remember: An activation of the sympathetic nervous system influences the disorders listed above, and a basic action of the Relaxation Response is to block the actions of the sympathetic nervous system. Drugs that perform similar actions—the so-called beta-blocking drugs and sympatholytic agents—are also used for these disorders. Not surprisingly, they are some of the most widely prescribed drugs in the Western world today. Inderal®, Corgard®, and Lopressor® are examples of commonly used drugs of this type. The Relaxation Response works in a directly related fashion on the ailment and its symptoms, but without the undesirable side effects of the drugs. On the contrary, the side effects of the Relaxation Response are feelings of peace and tranquillity.

The relative potency of the Relaxation Response compared with these drugs and the full extent of interaction between the Relaxation Response and these drugs remain to be studied. In the meantime, under your doctor's supervision the two can be used together. Your doctor can appropriately adjust your drug dosage. If he feels it is warranted, he can eliminate your drugs completely.

The usual sequence of events that can be expected, in my experience, is:

1. There is less concern about the symptoms or the illness; in other words, the anxiety cycle is broken.
2. The symptoms become less severe.
3. The symptoms are present less of the time and short periods of complete relief are noted.
4. The periods of relief become longer.
5. The symptoms are completely gone or remain in a fashion that no longer interferes with everyday activities. In fact, I have found that many patients have difficulty remembering their original symptoms.

The time duration for a person to experience these full benefits is quite variable. For some, it can be as short as one to two weeks. For others, up to a year is required. Most people can expect improvements to occur in approximately four to six weeks.

To demonstrate in practical terms how you can make use of the Faith Factor to achieve these results in your own life, I now want to turn to some specific applications and examples. Each is based on the fundamental Relaxation-Response technique described in the previous chapter. But it's important to tailor this technique somewhat to certain special situations.

Anxiety and Hyperventilation

We've all experienced anxiety reactions and their related symptoms of fright, panic, upset stomach, nausea, vomiting, diarrhea, constipation, shortness of breath, and inability to get along with others. You may feel that your stomach is "turning over" or "coming up into the throat," or that your heart is beating very rapidly.

Hyperventilation is often related to anxiety reactions. "Overbreathing" occurs, and it is associated with symptoms of shortness of breath, apprehension, dizziness, chest pains or chest tightness, difficulty in taking a deep breath, numbness in the limbs, palpitations, and spasms in the hands and feet. A classic treatment is to breathe into a paper bag for a short time.

There's another way of handling this specific problem and anxiety attacks in general, through a special application of the Relaxation Response. First of all, it's important that you be a regular practitioner of a technique that elicits the Response. This means you should follow on a consistent basis the steps outlined in the previous chapter:

1. Pick a focus word or phrase that is rooted in your personal belief system.
2. Sit quietly in a comfortable position.
3. Close your eyes.
4. Relax your muscles.
5. Become aware of your breathing, and breathe very slowly and naturally. Simultaneously, repeat your focus word or phrase as you exhale. Use one word or phrase during your sessions so that you'll automatically come to associate it with the calming impact of the Relaxation Response.
6. Assume a passive attitude, and if other thoughts intrude in your mind, gently disregard them.
7. Continue for ten to twenty minutes.
8. Practice the technique once or twice daily.

After you've followed this basic technique for several weeks, the likelihood of any anxiety reaction or of a hyperventilation attack will be diminished because you will have started to break the anxiety cycle. But when you feel an attack coming on, or if you find yourself in the midst of one, just say to yourself, "Okay, [your name], stop!" Then, take a deep breath and hold it. Breathe out very slowly and say silently to yourself the word, phrase, prayer, or sound that you normally use to elicit the Relaxation Response. Obviously, you shouldn't try to take such a breath in an inappropriate environment, such as at a sedate dinner party or in a business meeting, which might cause you some embarrassment (but you can often excuse yourself for a few moments quite easily).

I encountered one case of severe hyperventilation involving a fifty-nine-year-old, highly successful salesman. He hyperventilated—or "overbreathed"—in some tense situations, or even without any apparent reason. This led to dizziness, chest pains, tingling of his hands and fingers, and a sense of panic. Although he was a nonpracticing Catholic, I suggested that he use a prayer to elicit the Relaxation Response as the first part of his treatment. He said, "Thank you, doctor, for prescribing prayer. It's something I wanted to do, but I felt funny about it. But now that you, as a doctor, prescribe it, I'll do it."

After several weeks of eliciting the Relaxation Response in this fashion, he learned to control the hyperventilation. When he felt an attack coming on, he would simply say to himself, "John, cool it!" Then, he would take a deep breath and hold it, and as he exhaled, he would slowly recite his prayer. In this way, he became quite adept at aborting his attacks.

You should only repeat your focus word or phrase once or twice. If this doesn't work, just "bite the bullet" and cope in the best fashion you can. With time, however, this simple, deep-breath method and recalling to mind the focus word should stop the progression of anxiety attacks or hyperventilation.

Generally speaking, it's helpful in a situation like this if you have just one familiar focus word or phrase that you use all the time. If you shift back and forth between different words and prayers, they will not exert the same impact that one consistent term can have.

Improvement of Your Health

The same techniques that help to lessen and eventually do away with anxiety can also have a far broader impact on your health. They can break the anxiety cycle, which begins with anxiety, progresses into symptoms or progressive worsening of an illness, and culminates in more anxiety. Specifically, by using the basic Relaxation-Response technique described in the previous chapter in conjunction with your belief, you can provide effective treatment for the pain of headaches, backaches, angina pectoris, and other pains. Also, the Relaxation Response, enhanced by belief, can serve as treatment for diseases related to activation of the sympathetic nervous system. These maladies include hypertension, heart rate irregularities, and even the side effects of the treatment of cancer.

But let me again offer a word of caution here: I'm not suggesting, in any sense, that you should rely on the Faith Factor as advocated in this book to the exclusion of modern Western medical treatment, such as drugs or surgery.

Sometimes the Faith Factor can be powerful enough to do the job alone. In other cases, however, surgery or some medicinal treatment may well be in order. The Faith Factor can and does work well with other medical techniques. Your personal physician can guide you in selecting the combination of treatments that's best suited for your particular problem.

Having mentioned this qualification, though, I want to emphasize how important the Faith Factor can be in relieving many of your health problems. Remember that 75 percent of symptoms and diseases fit into the category that can be directly helped by the Faith Factor. Here are some supportive examples:

Headaches

The use of a Relaxation-Response technique to relieve headaches has been strikingly successful in many of my clinical experiences. For example, one thirty-six-year-old female social worker and homemaker suffered from migraine headaches three to four days a week that were so severe she sometimes had to stay in bed for full days in a darkened room. During these attacks, she was unable to care properly for her family or carry out the requirements of her job.

After she came for help, it became clear that the Faith Factor might be the best treatment. Since she was Jewish, I suggested she use the focus word *Shalom*. She began to practice the simple form of meditation we've already described in this book, and before long she became less concerned about her headaches, because even though they continued, they were much less severe. Next, the headaches recurred only about once a week. Now, on average, she has a mild headache about once every two months. She is able to work through them rather easily, both at home and on the job.

Another illustration of how the Faith Factor can relieve headaches involved a twelve-year-old boy who was also one of my patients. His parents told me that he used to cry all the time as an infant. When he became verbal, he was able to communicate to his parents that he had almost constant pain in his head. It turned out he had congenital migraines; in fact, there were few days that he didn't suffer from this problem. Sometimes the headaches were so severe that they prevented him from going to school for two to three days at a time. Also, he had great difficulty keeping up with his lessons because he missed so many classes and often could not study when he was at home.

The boy was a devout Catholic and he knew the Jesus Prayer: "Lord Jesus Christ, have mercy on me." So I suggested he use these words to elicit the Relaxation Response. He began to practice this meditation twice a day, and within two weeks, the intensity of the headaches lessened. Then he found that after two or three months he could "head off" his headaches when he felt the first twinges by reciting this prayer for ten to twenty minutes.

"Oh, when I see them coming, I sit down quietly and pray my prayer, and they just sort of melt away," he explained.

As a result, he has been able to start a relatively pain-free life for the first time.

Back Pain

The Relaxation-Response technique also works well with back pains. One thirty-two-year-old middle manager came to me with a severe low-back pain, which made it impossible for him to sit or stand for any length of time. He wasn't making any progress with standard medical therapies or medications. In fact, they seemed to be making his symptoms much worse. He became increasingly depressed, fearful, and lethargic. When I first saw him, he had sunk into a state of hopelessness.

I encouraged him to begin to elicit the Relaxation Response through regular, deep breathing. In this case, he didn't use a prayer because he was not religious. He used the number "one." But he had a basically self-assured outlook on life, which had enabled him to rise to a responsible position with his company. In short, he believed in himself—that he could do almost anything he set his mind to do. So, when he resolved to "succeed" with this meditative approach to his malady, he in effect introduced the Faith Factor, which for him centered on a belief in his inner strengths and abilities.

As a result, almost immediately he became less lethargic and less subject to feelings of hopelessness. Also, he became less afraid of his pain. Then, slowly, he became more active and involved in other aspects of his life. He also recognized that he could elicit the Relaxation Response with the pain still there and that he could get along all right with this approach. Now, although he is not totally pain-free, his pain is no longer a focal point of his life. He's able to carry on an essentially normal life, with occasional twinges of severe back pain. Also, he's less frightened of taking risks with his back pain. It took this young manager about twelve weeks to reach this level.

Chest Pain (Angina Pectoris)

Another physical problem that can be relieved or eliminated by the Faith Factor is angina pectoris, or the chest pains that are related to a heart disease. These pains may be brought on by excessive emotional activity, overeating, or exercise, and the classic way to find relief is to rest or take the drug nitroglycerin.

A sixty-nine-year-old black woman came to me with severe angina, which was the result of serious, underlying heart disease. She had been taking many medications for this problem, but still she experienced the pain three or four times daily, and it prevented her from carrying on with her normal life. She had originally heard me teaching the Relaxation Response to someone in the hospital bed next to her, and she asked if I thought there was any chance she might benefit from this technique.

I asked whether or not she was religious, and she said, "Indeed, I am. I'm a Christian." She chose a meditative prayer that was quite meaningful for her, "Jesus saves."

Then she used this prayer as her focus phrase, and immediately she started eliciting the Relaxation Response twice daily. This woman began to feel a sense of peace and quiet with this approach. Although she had to continue most of her medications because her disease was so severe, she is now mostly free of the angina pain, and she requires much less nitroglycerin. Also, she's increased her activity levels.

Hypertension

One of the most notable uses of the Relaxation Response has been its application to the problem of hypertension, or high blood pressure. Since the publication of my first book, *The Relaxation Response,* in 1975, thousands of people have used the Relaxation Response as treatment for hypertension. Usually, the way I treat such patients is to keep them on their medication, add a technique to elicit the Relaxation Response, and then as their blood pressure begins to decrease, I reduce the medications. In cases of mild hypertension, I've found that frequently I can do away completely with the medications. In virtually all cases, there is better control of blood pressure, with less medication.

But an additional problem that sometimes develops with hypertension patients is what's called the "cuff neurosis." This means that just the experience of having your blood pressure taken—including the anticipation of having the cuff placed around your upper arm—can elevate blood pressure. The worry and anxiety of having the measurement made creates an anxiety cycle centered on the measurement itself. One forty-four-year-old lawyer came to me because each time his blood pressure was measured, it seemed to get higher. When I saw him the readings were in the range of 180 over 110, which are quite high. Moreover, medication didn't work very well.

This man was not a religious person, but he was an avid jogger—one who believed this exercise could solve many of the problems of mankind. So I encouraged him to use his belief in exercise to get the maximum benefit out of the Relaxation Response. Specifically, we worked out a strategy by which he elicited the Relaxation Response while he jogged. He focused the cadence of his footsteps in a "one-two, one-two" rhythm for at least ten or twenty minutes during his exercise sessions. Within three weeks, his blood pressure came down to 140 over 90, and within twelve weeks, his blood pressure was within normal limits, at 120 over 80.

With many people who suffer from cuff neurosis, the fears begin two to three days before they come to see the physician. Their sympathetic nervous system is going at full blast, and their anxiety levels get higher and higher. Using the Relaxation Response, in conjunction with the person's belief system, can be highly effective in treating this problem.

Heartbeat and Cardiac Problems

The Faith Factor can also help to correct irregularities of the heartbeat and other cardiac problems. A retired shopkeeper, who was Greek Orthodox, came to see a colleague of mine and was found to be suffering from a very rapid heartbeat, which can sometimes be dangerous. Medications didn't seem to be working, so his doctor had suggested that he use the Relaxation Response. The doctor also told him to use the number "one" as his focus word, but when the man came back a few days later, he actually had gotten worse.

The doctor asked, "What's wrong with this technique?" The man replied, "It's like voodoo—like witchcraft."

Apparently, using the number "one" had connotations that conjured up negative rather than neutral or positive reactions in his thinking. So the doctor, after questioning the man in more detail about his personal beliefs, decided that the phrase *Kyrie eleison,* or "Lord, have mercy," would be better. Sure enough, when the man began to use these focus words, his bouts of rapid heartbeat began to slow down and soon were under control.

Cancer

The Relaxation Response can also enhance the possibilities that cancer patients may do better with their illness by breaking those mental stress "loops" that may cause them to have additional problems. For example, this technique is extremely useful in helping patients to overcome difficulties with nausea and vomiting from chemo-therapy for cancer.

One patient I know has cancer and needs chemotherapy treatments for it. She would frequently feel anxiety days before the treatment and also would experience panic, vomiting, and nausea during and after the chemotherapy. After a period of eliciting the Relaxation Response by focusing on her breathing, she found she was able to control her negative symptoms. She learned to meditate through the period when she was receiving the drugs.

Cholesterol Levels

Cholesterol levels can also be lowered by eliciting the Relaxation Response—especially if this phenomenon is combined with a person's deep personal beliefs. One study on this subject was conducted by Dr. Michael J. Cooper and Dr. Maurice M. Aygen and reported in the *Journal of Human Stress*. These researchers found that those using the Transcendental Meditation technique, which elicits the Re-laxation Response, were able to lower significantly the average cholesterol levels in their blood: Those levels dropped by as much as 35 percent. In contrast, the control group, who didn't practice any relaxation technique, expe-rienced no significant change in their cholesterol levels.

The technique used to treat these physical problems is, as I've stated, the same basic Relaxation-Response method with the faith-rooted focus word. But remember that in ap-plying this approach to physical problems, a passive atti-tude is vital. In other words, you can't "will" a headache, backache, or any other kind of illness to go away. In this regard, it's interesting to note that a Buddhist technique,

Herbert Benson, M.D.

far from fighting against painful symptoms to relieve pain, uses the pain itself as the focus word. This helps the individual create a passive attitude to the pain and thus helps break the anxiety cycle.

It's a mistake to try to direct the Faith Factor to operate in a certain way on a disease or disability. This active use of the will activates the sympathetic nervous system and in turn may cause or aggravate the problem, rather than improve it. In other words, the passive attitude that is associated with the Faith Factor will *allow* the problem to subside only when you stop trying so hard.

For these reasons, I'd suggest that you steer clear of any directive focus words, such as "heal" or "get better." If you concentrate too much on your physical problem and how your Relaxation-Response technique is working, your anxiety levels will increase rather than subside. That is, you'll only reinforce or start anew the anxiety cycles, rather than ease them.

On the other hand, despite the emphasis I place on being passive in eliciting the Relaxation Response, it's very important to *want* to get well so strongly that you can almost "taste" it. Like the cancer patients mentioned in a previous chapter, those who survive the longest and achieve the best health often have a strong desire to fight their disease. But this wanting to get well must not slip over into anxiety and worry if you should fail to improve at the rate you expect. The most effective attitude is more one of positive thinking, hope, and expectation than one of anxiety-producing concentration and monitoring.

After you assert your overwhelming desire to get well, back off. In other words, as you practice the elements that make possible the benefits of the Faith Factor, it's important to move from active desire to passive acceptance. In this way, you'll break the buildup of possible stress that performance-related positive thinking has engendered and prevent that stress from having a damaging effect on your body's natural healing capacities. What I'm saying is that there is a fine line between the health-promoting desire to get well and the stressful anxiety that can overtake that desire for health. The Faith Factor can help you maintain the balance that can lead to improved health.

I fully recognize how "un-Western" this advice is, but our experiences and data have documented its crucial importance. The advice, of course, poses a complicated challenge: You are doing something to get better or be made well, but you're being told not to care about how well your actions are working. My advice is to let your doctor do the necessary monitoring.

Insomnia

When you're asleep your body and mind work differently from when you're in a meditative state. Sleep and meditation each elicit different brain waves and different patterns of metabolism.

But even with these differences, it's quite easy to move from the Relaxation Response into sleep if you just alter your technique somewhat. As I've already mentioned, people often drift into sleep if they practice their technique while lying down. That's why we suggest that you assume only a moderately comfortable position when you want to use the Relaxation Response in the usual way.

But if you want to overcome chronic insomnia or just fall asleep during one particularly restless night, here's how you can combine the Faith Factor with your sleeping objective. First of all, practice a Relaxation-Response technique regularly. Then, after a week or two, when you are in bed and you wish to fall asleep or return to sleep after you've awakened:

1. Lie comfortably in bed.
2. Close your eyes.
3. Relax all your muscles. Start with your feet and progress to your calves, thighs, and abdomen, just as you do with the standard Relaxation-Response technique. Roll your head slowly and shrug your shoulders a few times to loosen up the related muscles.
4. Become aware of your breathing. As you breathe slowly and naturally, repeat silently your focus word or phrase as you exhale. For instance, you might exhale and think "Peace."
5. Slowly shift your attention to your abdomen. After a few minutes of breathing and repeating your word or phrase, notice how your abdomen expands as you breathe in. Do not repeat your focus word, but see how your abdomen also contracts as you exhale. Bring your attention to this rhythmic expansion and contraction of your abdomen.
6. Now direct your attention to what you feel in various parts of your body. For example, while you continue to focus on your breathing, become aware of what you are feeling in your right big toe. As you breathe out, focus your attention on the feelings of this toe. Then, on your next out-breath, focus on the feeling in your right second toe. On your next breath, focus on your right third toe. Then, progress to your right fourth and fifth toes, your right ankle, right calf, and right thigh—all the while sensing your rhythmic breathing patterns. Repeat this process with your left

toes and left leg, and then move up to your abdomen. Repeat the process, if necessary, starting with your right big toe.

7. Always maintain a passive attitude. As thoughts other than the awareness of your breathing or the feelings in your limbs come into your consciousness, think, "Oh, well." Then slowly redirect your attention. Frequently, people will begin to think, "Am I asleep yet? Why isn't the process working? When am I finally going to get to sleep?" Soon they get frustrated, and the anxiety cycle related to sleep will return. Because they're still awake, they discard the technique before it has had a chance to work. When such thoughts start to intrude, just return once more to an awareness of your breathing or to your focus word and start over.

One of the causes of insomnia is that we are occupied with all the concerns of today and what we think will be the worries of tomorrow. We keep our mind-body anxiety cycles operating. This kind of mental preoccupation is unproductive, in part because the thoughts that come into our minds late at night are usually mere fragments of ideas and concepts. Also, we are incapable of dealing adequately with them while we lie awake in bed because we lack the rest and perspective that help us with our problem-solving earlier in the day. How many problems that bothered you late at night have been forgotten or at least paled into insignificance with the coming of morning?

The Faith Factor used in this fashion can break these active worry or thought loops. You will then fall asleep as your bodily need for sleep takes over. Moreover, when your focus word or phrase is tied in to your belief system, your relaxing, sleep-inducing session can assume the form of a nighttime meditation or prayer. In this way, your practice can become much more important to you personally than just an insomnia treatment.

Use During Exercise

Many people regard choosing a Relaxation-Response technique and exercise as an either/or sort of thing. In other words, an aerobic runner who runs several miles every day may say, "Oh, I already work out for an hour or so daily. So I really don't have the time for this." Or there are those who have difficulty sitting quietly under any circumstances. But there's no need to choose one approach or the other, for they can be combined.

Some sports fit well with the Relaxation-Response techniques—especially the so-called aerobic activities like swimming or jogging. These athletic endeavors involve a rhythmic, smooth, repetitive kind of exercise that can enhance rather than detract from your ability to achieve a focused, passive frame of mind. The noncompetitive, individual activities can also become a helpful vehicle to allow you to break through the anxiety cycles of everyday thought.

Here's how this approach works in some common aerobic activities.

Jogging or Walking

1. If you are over forty or if you suffer from a physical ailment, first obtain your physician's advice.
2. Get into sufficiently good condition so that you can run or walk without becoming excessively short of breath or without suffering muscle fatigue for at least

thirty minutes of endurance activity. If you try to elicit the Relaxation Response when you first start your exercise program, much of your attention will be directed to how out of condition you feel.

3. Do your usual warm-up exercises before you run or walk.

4. As you jog or walk, keep your eyes open. Although the standard Relaxation-Response technique requires you to shut your eyes to avoid distractions, you have to see where you're going when you're combining this type of technique with exercise.

5. Become aware of your breathing. After you fall into a regular pattern of breathing, focus your attention on the in-and-out rhythm of your breath. As you breathe in, say to yourself silently, "in." When you exhale, think, "out." In effect, this becomes your mental device or focus word in the same way that you use your personal focus phrase with other Relaxation-Response methods.

If this rhythm is uncomfortable for you—for instance, if your breathing is too fast or too slow—you can focus on something else. For example, you can become aware of your feet hitting the ground. That is, you could silently alternate saying, "One . . . two . . . one . . . two."

Finally, there is, of course, nothing wrong with using a faith-oriented focus phrase or word during exercise. In fact, if you can find the right device, your running or walking experience will become even more enjoyable. I know of one high-ranking U.S. Army chaplain, a Catholic, who says the Jesus Prayer in rhythm to his exercises as he runs each day. But it's necessary to be more careful than you would normally be about the words you choose so that you maintain the rhythm of your movement. In other words, if your usual phrase doesn't fit the rhythm of your jogging, you may find the experience undesirable.

For example, if you silently say something like, "The peace that passes understanding," you may find that there are too many words and that you can't fit them all in perfectly with your movements. So you might want to select something shorter like, "Peace and joy."

6. Maintain a passive attitude. Just as you do with the standard Relaxation-Response techniques, gently disregard disruptive thoughts. Simply think to yourself, "Oh, well," and slip back into your repetitive focus word.

7. When you complete your set amount of exercise time, return to your normal after-exercise routine.

After running or jogging four or five miles, many experience a "high." With the concomitant use of a Relaxation-Response technique, this high usually occurs in the first or second mile. Also, we have found that when these techniques are utilized, exercise becomes more efficient. In other words, you can perform the same amount of exercise with less active metabolism. When we reported these changes in the medical literature, several marathon runners were upset because they felt we had given away a secret competitive technique they had been using.

Swimming

1. If you are over forty or if you suffer from a physical ailment, first obtain your physician's advice.

2. Get in physical condition before you try to employ the Faith Factor with swimming.
3. Do your normal warm-up exercises before you enter the water.
4. Keep your eyes open. As with jogging, you must be aware of the people around you. If you have access to an uncrowded pool where you can swim laps easily, so much the better. The fewer the distractions, the easier it will be to practice the method.
5. Become aware of your arms stroking through the water. As you get used to the rhythm of your arms slicing through the water, you can turn this awareness into your mental device. For example, every time you stroke with your right arm, think, "right." When you stroke with your left arm, think, "left." Or if you find it more comfortable, use your breathing as your device. That is, think "out" every time you exhale.

You may also want to use a focus word or phrase rooted in your personal beliefs to enhance the swimming experience still more. But as with jogging, be sure that you pick a device that will fit perfectly into the physical rhythm you've established.
6. Maintain a passive attitude. As distracting thoughts compete for your attention, gently disregard them and return to your awareness of your stroking and breathing.
7. Swim for your set period of time and then do your normal cool-down routine.

These jogging-walking and swimming instructions can be adapted to many different types of aerobic exercise. The basic approach can apply equally well to a stationary exercise bicycle or to a rowing machine, and with these two pieces of equipment, you might more easily ignore the injunctions against closing your eyes.

Almost any endurance exercise will fit into this approach as long as it doesn't demand your complete attention and unusual alertness. Clearly, handball, squash, or downhill skiing would be out of the question—and could even be dangerous if you failed to keep your mind on your activity. On the other hand, cross-country skiing, as physically demanding as it is, is suited to the use of a Relaxation-Response technique because the attention demands in many ways resemble the demands of jogging.

Concentration-oriented sports like tennis or golf or strenuous team activities like football or basketball require a great deal of active mental attention or explosive effort. Poor performance of these sports may even contribute to anxiety cycles, as the player fails to perform according to his personal standards. During the next performance, he may do worse. Many athletes find the regular use of Relaxation-Response techniques before competitions helps break this vicious cycle. Many use a prayer as their focus word.

There are a number of rhythmic exercises that also elicit the Relaxation Response. Notable are the various Chinese techniques such as T'ai Chi Ch'uan. These employ prescribed rhythmic movements with a passive attitude, relaxed muscles, and attention to breathing.

Creativity

Many times, a person can become inefficient in his work or develop mental blocks of one type or another if many pressures and concerns are bothering him. It's possible that the anxiety cycles are impeding his performance.

For example, I know one businessman who had to come

up with new business proposals for his job. But frequently he found he just couldn't focus properly for an extended period of time because he was always thinking about an upcoming negotiation or a disturbing recent phone conversation. I have another friend, a writer, who sometimes was dismayed because she couldn't come up with an appropriate lead, or first sentence or paragraph, for an article or book.

Both of these people have discovered that they can break loose from the "chains" of thinking in one set way or anxiety cycles and become more creative by using a variation on the Faith-Factor approach. The businessman finds that he can achieve this goal by using regularly the simple Relaxation-Response technique outlined in the previous chapter. He also keeps his creativity at a fine edge by being certain that he gets enough sleep—if necessary, by employing the anti-insomnia method I've outlined here.

As a general rule, he's more relaxed and flexible in his thinking simply as a result of his twice-a-day Relaxation-Response routine. I believe the Relaxation Response enhances creativity by breaking the unproductive "wired thinking loops" in the mind and allowing fresh associations to occur. It has been hypothesized that the new associations occur because new "wirings" are present.

As for the writer, she uses a similar technique, but because she affirms a traditional religious faith, she brings God more into the picture. In fact, she believes that her ideas and inspirations come directly from God, and so her meditation in a way takes on the form of ushering God into her life in a very direct way at various times during her day. She uses the phrase rooted in Catholicism "Come, Holy Spirit" in her Relaxation-Response sessions.

But it's important to note here that neither of these people uses the Relaxation-Response method in a directed way to break out of mental shackles. Rather, their creative freedom comes only when they "back off" from the problem, assume a passive attitude, and in effect say to themselves, "This problem is not all that important—if the answer comes, it comes; if it doesn't, it doesn't."

Robert M. Yerkes and John D. Dodson demonstrated in 1908 that as stress or anxiety increases, so do efficiency and performance. But this relation continues only to a certain level of anxiety. At some point, performance will decrease if the level of anxiety continues to increase. Since most of us have an excess of anxiety or stress, the way to increase performance is to back off.

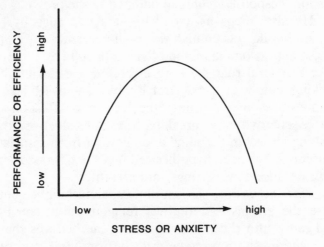

After you have been regularly eliciting the Relaxation Response, you will find it has become a part of you regardless of the technique you use. You'll also find it occurs spontaneously for a moment or two as you sit quietly. These mini Relaxation Responses can be brought forth at will, if you like. If you feel stressed or feel the beginning of an anxiety reaction, simply repeat your name and say, "Okay, (your name), stop." Then, take a deep breath and hold it, breathe out very slowly, and silently say your focus word to yourself. These instructions are, of course, the same as those utilized to stop an anxiety reaction.

These, then, are variations on the basic Relaxation-Response technique, enhanced by belief, which can bring the beneficial effects of the Faith Factor, more inner control, and better health. But do they mark just the beginning of the inner potential that is available to us? Just how far can human beings go in using their minds to control their bodies? And to take this question yet a step further: How far, if at all, can we go in using our minds to influence our outside environment? I want now to explore further the possible answers to these and other equally exciting questions.

9

||||||||||||||||||||||||||||||||

What are
the Outer Limits?

||||||||||||||||||||||||||||||||

Over the centuries many claims have been made about how far the mind can go in conquering matter. In part, what I've been attempting to do in my recent research is to try to determine just how much scientific validity there may be to some of these claims. My quest has been and continues to be an exploration of what may be the outer limits of our mental powers.

Of course, even as I use words like "mental" or "mind," I know it's not always clear exactly what they mean. For example, those with a religious faith or a philosophical world view that allows for some sort of extradimensional intervention in our three-dimensional reality may assume that the mind of a human being acts as a conduit for larger, cosmic forces. In other words, when a religious person utilizes meditative prayer, he may believe that the impact on his body—such as a lowering of his blood pressure or relief of his headache—is somehow tied in directly with the healing power of God.

On the other hand, the assumptions of the agnostic or atheist who experiences physical benefits from a nonreligious form of meditation may be quite different. He may believe that the mind means nothing more than the physical cells, chemical interactions, and electrical impulses that make up scientifically measurable brain activity.

In this book, as I've mentioned before, it has not been my purpose to try to determine which of these views is correct. If there is a supernatural source for some of our mental powers, I don't pretend to be in a position to evaluate which religion or faith orientation is superior to the next. Rather, I'm interested in the narrower question of what physical effects can be caused by certain mental activity, however "mental" may be defined.

But having mentioned this qualification, I will still say this: My study in this field has convinced me that, for whatever reason, faith does make a difference in enhancing the power of the mind over health and disease. In other words, the Faith Factor—or the combination of the Relaxation Response with a profound set of personal convictions—can provide at least two benefits not available through ordinary relaxation or meditative techniques: (1) It can encourage a person to be more persistent in following a regular Relaxation-Response program; and (2) it can combine the beneficial effects of the Relaxation Response with those of the placebo effect.

So faith does make a difference and can broaden a person's inner potential. But the question still remains: To what extent can a person with a well-developed faith, coupled with a meditation program, influence his body and perhaps even the world around him?

Recently I've been exploring some new areas of investigation that may throw light on just how far the human mind can go in changing or influencing physical reality. These center on faith-healing practices in a number of religious traditions and also the use of the mind to affect various realms of reality beyond the human body.

The Healing Question

Reports of healing practices through the invocation of magical or religious powers, energies, or forces have persisted for thousands of years. As I've mentioned elsewhere in this book, the ancient Egyptians named these energies *Ka,* the Hawaiians called them *Mana,* the Chinese use the term *Chi,* and the Indians use *Prana.* Healings were said to occur as far back as the third millennium B.C. among pilgrims who visited the tomb of the deified Imhotep, the chief physician, architect, and minister of the Egyptian ruler Zoser. Pilgrims also traveled for healing to temples in Greece, such as the one associated with Aesculapius.

In the Bible, healing was often associated with the healer's act of touching the diseased or crippled person. This approach later became identified in church tradition with the practice of "laying on of hands" in special healing services.

Also, a belief arose that temporal rulers, who were often thought to rule by divine right, possessed a special healing power in their touch. The Roman writer Pliny described Emperor Hadrian as having the ability to cure dropsy, or abnormal accumulations of fluid, with a touch. Similarly, the touch of English kings was widely employed in the treatment of scrofula, or tuberculosis of the lymph glands. For example, the chronicles of Edward the Confessor in the eleventh century record actual cures of scrofula after he laid his royal hands on the diseased areas. About two hundred years later, the household accounts of Edward I reported that on April 4, 1277, this monarch touched 73 people, and 288 on Easter of the same year.

The number of sick people touched by the kings of France was even larger. At one sitting Philip of Valois allegedly touched 1,500 people, and Louis XVI touched 2,400 at the time of his coronation in 1774.

How successful was this kingly touching in bringing about healings?

With the passage of time it's difficult to ascertain exactly how well these rulers did at curing diseases, and there was a considerable amount of English-French rivalry about the relative power of the touch of their kings. The competition even became as basic as trying to determine who first possessed the power. The French maintained it was Clovis I who initially used healing powers, just after his baptism in A.D. 496. The English, on the other hand, argued that the French kings had actually inherited this power from their English relatives.

The so-called king's touch persisted as late as 1824 when Charles X of France touched 121 people who were presented to him by the physicians Alibert and Dupuytren. In more recent times, Western civilization has viewed such healing sessions more skeptically—and even written them off as the work of quacks, witches, or charlatans.

But even today, healing practices similar to those of earlier times continue in our society, and extravagant claims are sometimes made about what's possible. I became personally interested in these modern-day healings after receiving letters or visits from individuals who claimed their healing powers were directly related to their own elicitation of the Relaxation Response. A number of those who contacted me said the Relaxation Response was an essential element and allowed them to become channels or conduits for various healing forces. They asked me to start the study of healing so that they could learn more about what they were doing. Since I had defined a component of healing—that is, the Relaxation Response—they suggested I take another step. I decided to examine what was known about this healing phenomenon.

After a considerable amount of study, I approach faith-healing practices by dividing them into three categories: (1) self-willed healings; (2) healings that are dependent upon the presence of a healer; and (3) healings that occur without the person who is being healed willing it and without the presence of the healer, or those occurring in plants and animals. Now, I want first to examine categories 1 and 2 together in light of the placebo effect. Then, I'll consider the broader issues involved in category 3.

Healing and the Placebo Effect

The first two types of healings—those that are self-willed and those that involve the actual presence of a healer—can be understood, at least in part, in terms of the so-called placebo effect, which I've already discussed in previous chapters. The placebo effect, you'll recall, refers to the changes produced by beliefs and expectations and through interpersonal relationships.

The broad definition of the placebo effect that I prefer to

use is this: It's the effect of any therapeutic procedure or substance that lacks the *specific* power to help a condition being treated.

Suppose you're suffering from a severe headache, and the person treating you gives you medicine that has been shown to have a specific action on infections—let's say, an antibiotic. From the usual medical viewpoint, however, the medicine has never been shown to have any effect on headaches. But the person still tells you that the medicine will definitely relieve your headache, and indeed it does. In this case, the antibiotic would be operating as a placebo and through the placebo effect would produce a change—namely, the relief of your headache.

As I've shown before, the placebo effect results from a combination of factors involving the patient, the physician, and importantly, the relationship between the two. Furthermore, the belief system of the patient is of primary importance in triggering the placebo effect. That is, patients who believe that a treatment will be effective are much more likely to benefit.

The thoughts and the behavior of the healer or physician are also supremely important in the working of the placebo effect. Those healers who are attentive to the needs of the patient, who are self-confident and have faith in the effectiveness of their treatments, are much more likely to cause the positive placebo effect to come into play. In this regard, Hippocrates said, ". . . some patients, though conscious that their condition is perilous, recover their health simply through their contentment with the goodness of the physician."

In addition to utilizing the placebo effect, healers make use of the Relaxation Response. Those who are able to overcome diseases and emotional disorders through nonmedical means have been shown to elicit the Relaxation Response frequently during the practice of their art. In most cases, the healer associates his altered state of consciousness, which occurs when the Relaxation Response is elicited, with the onset of the healing event.

Generally speaking, the initial step in this process is for the healer to employ a mental technique to quiet his or her mind. For example, in Brian Inglis's book *Fringe Medicine,* the technique of the British spiritual healer Harry Edwards is described this way: "For the healing power to begin to operate, he found that he must avoid the temptation to concentrate: 'It is not a mental concentration that is needed, but mental abandonment . . . the ideal to be arrived at is a stage of mental meditation, with the directive of seeking contact with a spirit'. . . ."

The purpose of eliciting the Relaxation Response by such techniques is to reach "attunement" with the person being healed so that the healing powers, forces, or energies will pass through the subject. Or as Edwards puts it, "The healer feels a sympathy for him or her and then tends to 'blend in' with the patient. After inducing in them a relaxed state, it is well for the healer to spend just a moment to deepen his attunement with both spirit and patient. By this, we have the perfect state of healer attuned to spirit and to patient, bringing about a state of 'oneness' with all three."

Along these same lines, Lawrence LeShan in *The Medium, the Mystic and the Physicist* says that the healer must experience an altered state of consciousness in which he views himself and the person being healed as one entity. Also, a passive attitude is essential. "There is no attempt to 'do anything' to the healee, but simply to meet him, to be one with him, to unite with him."

Reports such as these, which indicate that healers may

experience the Relaxation Response, suggest that the Faith Factor could well be at work in some instances of healing where dramatic physical improvements or recoveries occur. In other words, the prayers and encouraging words as well as a quieting calmness during the healing process may encourage the person's belief system to begin to break the harmful loops of thinking and anxiety cycles that are hindering recovery or causing the illness. The degree to which healings by the spiritual healers are the result of the use of the placebo effect or the result of possible outside forces or energies is an issue that can't be determined, given the present state of our medical knowledge and technical expertise. Until the alleged outside energies can be measured or their effects identified independently of the presence of the placebo effect, their presence cannot be scientifically proved.

The Most Puzzling Kind of Healing

Therefore, it's possible, at least to some extent, to explain the first two kinds of healing in medical terms through the placebo effect. But the third kind of healing—the type that occurs without the subject willing to be healed and without the healer being present, or that which occurs in plants or animals—presents greater difficulty. In these cases, the healer has to work from afar; the belief of the subject is not a factor; and there's no possibility of beneficial personal interaction between the two. Or as far as plants and animals are concerned, they don't know that a healing is expected. Hence, there's no room for the placebo effect as we know it to operate.

In such a case, certain controlled experiments involving

plants and animals have been performed in an attempt to determine the action of forces, energies, or powers that are channeled through the healer. One of the few investigators to perform controlled experiments of healing on plants and animals is Dr. Bernard Grad of Montreal, Canada. He conducted all his experiments with one man, a "Mr. E," who, according to Grad, "claimed to have observed healings in people and animals on whom he had practiced the laying on of hands."

One experiment involved the surgical removal of areas of the skin of mice. The animals were then divided into three groups of sixteen animals each, and there was no statistically significant difference in the size of the wounds in the three groups. One group was exposed to "laying on of hands" by Mr. E. Another group was heated artificially to the same hand temperature and for the same amount of time as the animals exposed to the heat of Mr. E's hands. The third group had no exposure to Mr. E, and they were not heated.

The results? Eleven days after the wounds were inflicted, the wounds of the group exposed to Mr. E were significantly smaller than those in the other two groups.

In a more elaborate experiment, Grad and his associates caused surgical skin wounds on three hundred mice. Then the animals were divided into three groups according to weight, age, general health, and wound size. One group was exposed to Mr. E's touch. Another was exposed to the hands of medical students who claimed no healing abilities. The third group received no special treatment.

During the treatment periods, the mice were put in cages that were placed inside opaque paper bags. Half of the bags in each group were stapled closed, and the other half were left open. In the half left open, Mr E and the medical students inserted their hands without looking at the mice or the cage. In the closed bags, the hands were placed upon the bag itself.

On the fifteenth and sixteenth days after the wounding was performed, the mean surface area of the wounds of the animals in the open bags was significantly smaller for those exposed to Mr. E than for those in the other two groups. Also, although the size of the healing wounds didn't vary significantly for the mice in the closed bags, their mean wound areas were somewhat smaller in the group exposed to Mr. E.

In some plant experiments, Grad studied Mr. E's influence upon barley seed growth. Twenty barley seeds were planted in each of twenty-four pots by Mr. E, and the pots were then divided into two equal groups. Next, Mr. E "treated" a one percent saline solution this way: He held open beakers between his hands for fifteen minutes by supporting each of them with his left hand from below and suspending his right hand three to four centimeters over the surface. Another "control" saline solution—one that was untreated by Mr. E—was then prepared in exactly the same way but without Mr. E's presence. Finally, the saline in these two sets of beakers was coded and given to Grad. Grad himself watered the equally divided pots, without knowing which solution had been treated by Mr. E.

Here's what happened: The seeds that received the treated saline yielded significantly more plants on day seven, but not on days eight to thirteen. Also, the treated plants grew higher than those untreated on days eight, nine, eleven, twelve, and thirteen. Finally, the pots that received the treated saline yielded significantly more plant material on days eight, nine, eleven, twelve, and thirteen. When this experiment was repeated exactly, but without Mr. E treating the saline, no significant differences were found between the groups in the second experiment.

Subsequently, Grad performed four more experiments with Mr. E and barley seed growth. Each of these experiments employed elaborate "double blind" procedures to ensure proper controls. After Mr. E "treated" one of two stoppered bottles of saline that were enclosed within paper bags, the seedlings were watered by an individual who did not know which bottle was so treated. In three of these four experiments, there was once again significantly enhanced growth only in the seeds watered with the Mr. E-treated saline.

Unfortunately, the animal and plant experiments of Grad have not been repeated. In the scientific method, repeating an experiment by another investigator and obtaining similar results is a necessary process to ensure validity. Indeed, I am familiar with work that has yielded findings akin to those of Grad. But when the scientists attempted to replicate their own findings, they found different, nonsupportive results. Without a consistency of data, they chose not to report their findings because the results could be explained on the basis of probabilities.

If ever proved valid, Grad's investigations would suggest that there may indeed be healing forces, energies, or powers that are now poorly understood by modern scientists. His work, if verifiable, points to the effects of these phenomena, but in no way defines them. So far, there are few studies that attempt to measure such forces, energies, or powers. When scientists, using sensitive, modern detectors of energy, have tried to make these measurements, no energy could be detected. Indeed, there is little within the framework of modern physics that even allows for the presence of such forces.

What, then, are we to make of reports of healing in humans? Clearly, mere *belief* in a therapeutic system—like a medicine, surgical procedure, or other treatment—enhances the healing power of such a system through the placebo effect. We've seen this in a variety of ways throughout this book.

But is it possible there may be more at work in some cases than just the placebo effect? I had the opportunity to witness the possible presence of unusual forces during some of my meetings with disciples of the Dalai Lama. You'll remember that one of the reasons I traveled to India was to see whether claims of levitation, or floating off the ground, were valid. If levitation were possible, it would be clear evidence of a force that could counteract gravity. We had established that the advanced meditational practice of *gTum-mo* Yoga could raise skin temperature. Would other meditational practices demonstrate levitation?

Because of the approval of the Dalai Lama, we were allowed to witness the practice of *lung gom-pa*. This advanced meditative practice entailed levitation, or translated literally, the ability to "go up and down." Several monks who practiced *lung gom-pa* met us at a hotel in the Indian Himalayas in a small town called Chail. The hotel was formerly one of the many palaces of a renowned, extraordinarily wealthy, high-living Indian ruler, the Maharajadhiraj of Patiala. Our meetings took place in one of the enormous bedrooms that had been used by one of his several hundred wives.

Before we were allowed to view the practice of *lung*

gom-pa, it was necessary first to be initiated. When the monks took their vows, they were told that if they disclosed their practices to the uninitiated, both they and their viewers would go to hell forever. Accordingly, the Dalai Lama's intercession permitted us to be initiated through listening to the recital of Buddhist scriptures.

Two monks, the Venerable K.G., aged seventy, and the Venerable T.P., aged thirty-four, then demonstrated their practice. They dressed only in loincloths and sat in a cross-legged position upon a small pile of carpets. They carried out a number of physical exercises in unison, including deep breathing; slapping their hands against their own chests, arms, and legs; and swaying. As these were performed, they chanted. They stood, rapidly crossed their legs into a cross-legged position, and fell to the ground with their legs remaining crossed. As they landed on the carpets, they slapped the outer portions of their legs outward and downward, thus creating a very loud noise. Then, as they sat cross-legged, they sucked their abdomens into their rib cages and produced a large cavity below their ribs. At this point, the older monk said that the younger would proceed alone because what was to follow was too strenuous for his age.

The young monk stood, bent his knees slightly, and jumped three to four feet into the air, with his legs straight. While in the air, he rapidly assumed the cross-legged position and fell to the ground while maintaining this position. He landed with a resounding crash as he slapped his crossed legs outward and downward. The monks completed their ritual by sitting together and apparently repeating many of their previous actions.

We asked whether what we had seen was the so-called "levitation meditation" and were told that indeed it was.

We had witnessed a remarkable athletic performance, but there was no floating or hovering. The fact that only the younger monk could perform the exercise also suggested it was athletic, not spiritual. If spiritual, one would have suspected the older monk would be more proficient.

I later asked them whether it was possible to stay up in the air. The younger monk said his great-grandfather had been able to do so, but he knew of no one doing it today. I then asked the older man if he knew of anyone who could carry out such a feat. He said it was an ability that was present many hundreds of years ago but not today. I asked the older monk if he would like to levitate, and with a twinkle in his eyes, he responded, "There is no need. We now have airplanes."

We later tested the ability of these monks to raise skin temperature during their practice of *gTum-mo* Yoga. The results replicated and extended what we had noted in the three monks who lived in and around Upper Dharmsala. Therefore, we verified a remarkable mind-body capacity, but we did not find any evidence to substantiate the presence of a hitherto undescribed power.

It seems to me that the experiments with plants and animals that claim the presence of healing energies, forces, or powers should be repeated with other healers. By simply refusing to believe that healing can occur outside normal, known scientific channels, we lessen the probability of our understanding what is involved in the healing process. Further, open-minded investigations might reveal exciting and useful information about such reported mind-body possibilities as:

- The scientific basis for at least some instances of faith-healing. Probably, many of these healings can be explained through the operation of the placebo effect. If so, we should then work to understand better the placebo effect.

- A new understanding of where scientific inquiry must end and where the exploration or acceptance of some sort of spiritual reality should begin
- The scientific basis, if any, for the reported miracles that have occurred at the Roman Catholic shrine of Lourdes and other such holy places
- The medical implications of healings that have been reported in recent years among Protestant groups such as the Vineyard Christian Fellowship, which is pastored by John Wimber of the Fuller Evangelistic Association in southern California. In that congregation, there have been many published reports of miraculous healings of the sick.

The quest that I've described in this book—the search for the link between the power of belief and its practical effect on physical reality—should continue then on many fronts. What has been presented as the Faith Factor is just one part of an ongoing discovery process, one that will gradually roll back the limits of what we know as "science" and should give us a deeper understanding of the broad implications of what we accept as personal faith or belief.

As a Western physician, I can only report and accept what I can measure scientifically. But our horizons, which delineate the powers of the body, mind, and spirit, as well as our scientific potential for the future, can only expand. We should allow ourselves to speculate about the extraordinary, to explore the unlikely, and even to hope for what is now believed to be impossible.

Bibliography

Chapter 1

The Holy Bible. Old and New Testaments in the King James Version. Nashville, New York: Regency Publishing House, 1970.

Benson, H. *The Relaxation Response.* New York: William Morrow, 1975.

Benson, H. *The Mind/Body Effect.* New York: Simon & Schuster, 1979.

Chapter 2

Aldrich, C. K. "A Case of Recurrent Pseudocyesis." *Perspectives in Biology and Medicine* 16 (1972), pp. 11–21.

Armstrong, R. H., et al. "Dreams and Gastric Secretions in Duodenal Ulcer Patients." *The New Physician* 14 (1965), pp. 241–243.

Bivin, G. D., and Klinger, M. P. *Pseudocyesis.* Bloomington: Principia Press, 1937.

Capra, F. *The Tao of Physics.* Boulder, Colorado: Shambhala Publications, Inc., 1975.

Fried, P. H., et al. "Pseudocyesis: A Psychosomatic Study in Gynecology." *Journal of the American Medical Association* 145 (1951), pp. 1329–1335.

Fry, J. *Profiles of Disease: A Study in the Natural History of Common Disease.* Edinburgh: E. and S. Livingstone, 1966.

Harth, E. *Windows of the Mind: Reflections of the Physical Basis of Consciousness.* New York: William Morrow, 1982.

Hippocrates. *Oeuvres Complètes.* Paris: Baliere, 1937.

Hunt, M. *The Universe Within: A New Science Explores the Mind.* New York: Simon & Schuster, 1982.

Ingelfinger, F. J. "Medicine: Meritorious or Meretricious." *Science* 200 (1978), pp. 942–946.

Knight, J. A. "False Pregnancy in a Male." *Psychosomatic Medicine* 22 (1960), pp. 260–266.

Kroger, W. S. *Psychosomatic Obstetrics, Gynecology and Endocrinology.* Springfield, Illinois: Charles C. Thomas, 1962.

MacWilliams, J. A. "Some Applications of Physiology to Medicine. III. Blood Pressure and Heart Rate Action during Sleep and Dreams." *British Medical Journal* 22 (1923), pp. 1195–1200.

Murao, S., et al. "All-night Polygraphic Studies of Nocturnal Angina Pectoris." *Japanese Heart Journal* 13 (1972), pp. 295–306.

Murray, J. L., and Abraham, G. E. "Pseudocyesis: A Review." *Obstetrics and Gynecology* 51 (1978), pp. 627–631.

Nowlin, J. B., et al. "The Association of Nocturnal Angina Pectoris with Dreaming." *Annals of Internal Medicine* 63 (1965), pp. 1040–1046.

Reinis, S., and Goldman, J. M. *The Chemistry of Behavior: A Molecular Approach to Neuronal Plasticity.* New York: Plenum, 1982.

Torrance, T. F. *Space, Time and Incarnation.* New York: Oxford University Press, 1978.

Zukav, G. *The Dancing Wu Li Masters.* New York: William Morrow, 1979.

Chapter 3

Benson, H. "Body Temperature Changes during the Practice of gTum-mo Yoga." (Matters Arising) *Nature* 298 (1982), p. 402.

Benson, H., and Epstein, M. D. "The Placebo Effect—A Neglected Asset in the Care of Patients." *Journal of the American Medical Association* 232 (1975), pp. 1225–1227.

Benson, H., et al. "Body Temperature Changes during the Practice of gTum-mo (Heat) Yoga." *Nature* 295 (1982), pp. 234–236.

Benson, H., and McCallie, D. P., Jr. "Angina Pectoris and the Placebo Effect." *New England Journal of Medicine* 300 (1979), pp. 1424–1429.

Butterfield, F. *China: Alive in the Bitter Sea.* New York: Times Books, 1982.

Dana, H. W. L. "In the Southeast Corner." *Harvard Alumni Bulletin* 48 (1946), pp. 575–579.

David-Neel, A. *Magic and Mystery in Tibet.* New York: Penguin Books, 1971.

Chapter 4

Anonymous. "Geshe, Doctor of Philosophy." *News Tibet* 18 (1983), pp. 9–10.

Benson, H. "Body Temperature Changes during the Practice of gTum-mo Yoga." (Matters Arising) *Nature* 298 (1982), p. 402.

Benson, H., et al. "Body Temperature Changes during the Practice of gTum-mo (Heat) Yoga." *Nature* 295 (1982), pp. 234–236.

Chapter 5

Abeloff, M. D., and Derogatis, L. R. "Psychologic Aspects of the Management of Primary and Metastatic Breast Cancer." *Progress in Clinical and Biological Research* 12 (1977), pp. 505–516.

Anonymous. "Epidemic Hysteria." *British Medical Journal* 1 (1979), pp. 408–409.

Benson, H., and Epstein, M. D. "The Placebo Effect—A Neglected Asset in the Care of Patients." *Journal of the American Medical Association* 232 (1975), pp. 1225–1227.

Benson, H., and McCallie, D. P., Jr. "Angina Pectoris and the Placebo Effect." *New England Journal of Medicine* 300 (1979), pp. 1424–1429.

Blumberg, E. M., West, P. M., and Ellis, F. W. "A Possible Relationship Between Psychological Factors and Human Cancer." *Psychosomatic Medicine* 16 (1954), pp. 277–286.

Borysenko, J. "Behavioral-Physiological Factors in the Development and Management of Cancer." *General Hospital Psychiatry* 4 (1982), pp. 69–74.

Brody, J. E. "Deficiencies of Vitamins." *The New York Times Magazine* 130 (1981), pp. 58–63.

Colligan, M. J., et al. "An Investigation of Apparent Mass Psychogenic Illness in an Electronics Plant." *Journal of Behavioral Medicine* 2 (1979), pp. 297–309.

Cornish, J. "Remarkable Effects of Fanaticism on the Inhabitants of Several Towns in Cornwall." *Medical and Physical Journal* 31 (1814), pp. 373–379.

Davidson, A. "Choreomania: An Historical Sketch with Some Account of an Epidemic Observed in Madagascar." *Edinburgh Medical Journal* 131 (1867), pp. 124–136.

Davy, R. B. "St. Vitus' Dance and Kindred Affections." *The Cincinnati Lancet and Clinic* 4 (1880), pp. 440–445.

Dimond, E. G., Kittle, C. F., and Crockett, J. E. "Comparison of Internal Mammary Artery Ligation and Sham Operation for Angina Pectoris." *American Journal of Cardiology* 5 (1960), pp. 483–486.

Egbert, L. D., et al. "Reduction of Postoperative Pain by Encouragement and Instruction of Patients." *New England Jour-*

nal of Medicine 270 (1964), pp. 825–827.

George, J. M., et al. "The Effects of Psychological Factors and Physical Trauma on Recovery from Oral Surgery." *Journal of Behavioral Medicine* 3 (1980), pp. 291–310.

Greer, S., Morris, T., and Pettingale, K. W. "Psychological Response to Breast Cancer: Effect on Outcome." *Lancet* 13 (1979), pp. 785–787.

Ikemi, Y., et al. "Psychosomatic Consideration of Cancer Patients Who Have Made a Narrow Escape from Death." *Dynamic Psychiatry* 8 (1975), pp. 77–93.

Ingelfinger, F. "Medicine: Meritorious or Meretricious." *Science* 200 (1978), pp. 942–946.

Kennedy, B. J., et al. "Psychological Response of Patients Cured of Advanced Cancer." *Cancer* 38 (1976), pp. 2184–2191.

Luparello, T., et al. "Influences of Suggestion on Airway Reactivity in Asthmatic Subjects." *Psychosomatic Medicine* 30 (1968), pp. 819–825.

Markush, R. E. "Mental Epidemics: A Review of the Old to Prepare for the New." *Public Health Reviews* 2 (1973), pp. 353–442.

Martin, A. "History of the Dancing Mania: A Contribution to the Study of Psychic Mass Infection." *American Journal of Clinical Medicine* 30 (1923), pp. 265–271.

Massey, E. W., Brannon, W. L., and Riley, T. L. "The 'Jerks': Mass Hysteria or Epilepsy?" *Southern Medical Journal* 74 (1981), pp. 607–609.

McFadden, E. R., Jr., et al. "The Mechanism of Action of Suggestion in the Induction of Acute Asthma Attacks." *Psychosomatic Medicine* 31 (1969), pp. 134–143.

McLeod, W. R. "Merphos Poisoning or Mass Panic?" *Australian and New Zealand Journal of Psychiatry* 9 (1975), pp. 225–229.

Rosen, G. "Psychopathology in the Social Process: Dance Frenzies, Demonic Possession, Revival Movements and Similar So-Called Psychic Epidemics." *Bulletin of the History of Medicine* 36 (1962), pp. 13–44.

Sosa, R., et al. "The Effect of a Supportive Companion on Perinatal Problems, Length of Labor, and Mother-Infant Interaction." *New England Journal of Medicine* 303 (1980), pp. 597–600.

Stravraky, K. M., et al. "Psychological Factors in the Outcome of Human Cancer." *Journal of Psychosomatic Research* 12 (1968), pp. 251–259.

Thomas, K. *Religion and the Decline of Magic.* New York: Charles Scribner's Sons, 1971.

Weisman, A. D., Worden, J. W., and Sobel, H. J. *Psychological Screening and Intervention with Cancer Patients. A Research Report.* Boston: Massachusetts General Hospital, 1980.

Chapter 6

Benson, H., and Epstein, M. D. "The Placebo Effect—A Neglected Asset in the Care of Patients." *Journal of the American Medical Association* 232 (1975), pp. 1225–1227.

Benson, H., and McCallie, D. P., Jr. "Angina Pectoris and the Placebo Effect." *New England Journal of Medicine* 300 (1979), pp. 1424–1429.

Bok, S. "The Ethics of Giving Placebos." *Scientific American* 231 (1974), pp. 17–23.

Bok, S. "White Lies." In *Lying: Moral Choice in Public and Private Life,* pp. 66–88. New York: Pantheon Books, 1978.

Couch, N. P., et al. "The High Cost of Low-frequency Events. The Anatomy and Economics of Surgical Mishaps." *New England Journal of Medicine* 304 (1981), pp. 634–637.

Freis, E. D. "Should Mild Hypertension Be Treated?" *New England Journal of Medicine* 307 (1982), pp. 306–309.

Hammond, S. *We Are All Healers.* New York: Ballantine Books, 1973.

Hoffman, J. W., et al. "Reduced Sympathetic Nervous System Responsivity Associated with the Relaxation Response." *Science* 215 (1982), pp. 190–192.

Holmes, O. W. *The Works of Oliver Wendell Holmes,* Vol. 9, *Medical Essays.* Boston: Houghton Mifflin, 1892.

Kaplan, N. M. "Mild Hypertension. When and How to Treat." *Archives of Internal Medicine* 143 (1983), pp. 255–259.

Kaplan, N. M. "New Approaches to the Therapy of Hypertension." *American Journal of Cardiology* 51 (1983), pp. 621–627.

Kaplan, N. M. "Therapy for Mild Hypertension. Toward a More Balanced View." *Journal of the American Medical Association* 249 (1983), 365–367.

Kaufman, J., et al. *Over the Counter Pills That Don't Work.* Washington, D.C.: Public Citizen's Health Research Group, 1983.

Lehmann, J. W., and Benson, H. "Nonpharmacologic Therapy of Blood Pressure." *General Hospital Psychiatry* 4 (1982), pp. 27–32.

Lehmann, J. W., and Benson, H. "The Behavioral Treatment of Hypertension." In *Hypertension: Physiopathology and Treatment,* eds. J. Genest, et al. New York: McGraw-Hill, 1983.

Pickering, T. G. "Treatment of Mild Hypertension and the Reduction of Cardiovascular Mortality: The 'Of or By' Dilemma." *Journal of the American Medical Association* 249 (1983), pp. 399–400.

Regestein, Q. R. *Sound Sleep.* New York: Simon & Schuster, 1980.

Wolfe, S. M., Coley, C. M., and the Health Research Group. *Pills That Don't Work.* Washington, D.C.: Public Citizen's Health Research Group, 1981.

Chapter 7

The Catholic Encyclopedia. Eds. C. G. Herbermann, et al. New York: Robert Appleton Company, 1907.

The Holy Bible. Old and New Testaments in the King James Version. Nashville, New York: Regency Publishing House, 1970.

Beary, J. F., and Benson, H. "A Simple Psychophysiologic Technique Which Elicits the Hypometabolic Changes of the Relaxation Response." *Psychosomatic Medicine* 36 (1974), pp. 115–120.

Benson, H. *The Relaxation Response.* New York: William Morrow, 1975.

Benson, H., Beary, J. F., and Carol, M. P. "The Relaxation Response." *Psychiatry* 37 (1974), pp. 37–46.

Benson, H., et al. "Continuous Measurement of O_2 Consumption and CO_2 Elimination during a Wakeful Hypometabolic State." *Journal of Human Stress* 1 (1975), pp. 37–44.

Jevning, R., et al. "Redistribution of Blood Flow in Acute Hypometabolic Behavior." *American Journal of Physiology* 235 (1978), pp. 89–92.

Philips, A. Th. *Daily Prayers with English Translation.* New York: Hebrew Publishing Co.

Smith, H. *The Religions of Man.* New York: Harper & Row, 1958.

Wallace, R. K., Benson, H., and Wilson, A. F. "A Wakeful Hypometabolic Physiologic State." *American Journal of Physiology* 221 (1971), pp. 795–799.

Chapter 8

Benson, H. "Systemic Hypertension and the Relaxation Response." *New England Journal of Medicine* 296 (1977), pp. 1152–1156.

Benson, H. "The Relaxation Response: History, Physiologic Basis and Clinical Usefulness." *Acta Medica Scandinavica* (Supplementum) 660 (1982), pp. 231–237.

Benson H. "Your Innate Asset for Combatting Stress." *Harvard Business Review* 52 (1974), pp. 49–60.

Benson, H., and Allen, R. L. "How Much Stress Is Too Much?" *Harvard Business Review* 58 (1980), pp. 86–92.

Benson, H., Alexander, S., and Feldman, C. L. "Decreased Premature Ventricular Contractions through the Use of the Relaxation Response in Patients with Stable Ischemic Heart Disease." *Lancet* ii (1975), pp. 380–382.

Benson, H., Dryer, T., and Hartley, L. H. "Decreased Oxygen Consumption during Exercise with Elicitation of the Relaxation Response." *Journal of Human Stress* 4 (1978), pp. 38–42.

Benson, H., et al. "Treatment of Anxiety: A Comparison of the Usefulness of Self-Hypnosis and a Meditational Relaxation Technique." *Psychotherapy and Psychosomatics* 30 (1978), pp. 229–242.

Benson, H., Klemchuk, H. P., and Graham, J. R. "The Usefulness of the Relaxation Response in the Therapy of Headache." *Headache* 14 (1974), pp. 49–52.

Benson, H., Pomeranz, B., and Kutz, I. "The Relaxation Response and Pain." In *Textbook of Pain,* eds. P. D. Wall and R. Melzack. London: Churchill Livingstone, 1984.

Benson, H., et al. "Decreased Blood Pressure in Borderline Hypertensive Subjects Who Practiced Meditation." *Journal of Chronic Diseases* 27 (1974), pp. 163–169.

Benson, H., et al. "Decreased Blood Pressure in Pharmacologically Treated Hypertensive Patients Who Regularly Elicited the Relaxation Response." *Lancet* i (1974), pp. 289–291.

Carrington, P., et al. "The Use of Meditation-Relaxation Techniques for the Management of Stress in a Working Population." *Journal of Occupational Medicine* 22 (1980), pp. 221–231.

Cooper, M. J., and Aygen, M. M. "A Relaxation Technique in the Management of Hypercholesteremia." *Journal of Human Stress* 5 (1979), pp. 24–27.

Gutmann, M. C., and Benson, H. "Interaction of Environmental Factors and Systemic Arterial Blood Pressure: A Review." *Medicine* 50 (1971), pp. 543–553.

Hoffman, J. W., et al. "Reduced Sympathetic Nervous System Responsivity Associated with the Relaxation Response." *Science* 215 (1982), pp. 190–192.

Kabat-Zinn, J. "An Outpatient Program in Behavioral Medicine for Chronic Pain Patients Based on the Practice of Mindfulness Meditation: Theoretical Considerations and Preliminary Results." *General Hospital Psychiatry* 4 (1982), pp. 33–47.

Lehmann, J. W., and Benson, H. "Nonpharmacologic Therapy of Blood Pressure." *General Hospital Psychiatry* 4 (1982), pp. 27–32.

Bibliography

Lehmann, J. W., and Benson, H. "The Behavioral Treatment of Hypertension." In *Hypertension: Physiopathology and Treatment,* eds. J. Genest, et al. New York: McGraw-Hill, 1983.

Lown, B., et al. "Basis for Recurring Ventricular Fibrillation in the Absence of Coronary Artery Disease and Its Management." *New England Journal of Medicine* 294 (1976), pp. 623–629.

MacCallum, M. J. "The Transcendental Meditation Program and Creativity." In *Scientific Research on the Transcendental Meditation Program. Collected Papers,* Vol. I, eds. W. Orme-Johnson and J. T. Farrow, pp. 410-414. West Germany: MERU Press, 1977.

Morrow, G. R., and Morrell, C. "Behavioral Treatment of the Anticipatory Nausea and Vomiting Induced by Cancer Chemotherapy." *New England Journal of Medicine* 307 (1982), pp. 1476–1480.

Peters, R. K., and Benson, H. "Time Out from Tension." *Harvard Business Review* 56 (1978), pp. 120–124.

Peters, R. K., Benson, H., and Peters, J. M. "Daily Relaxation Response Breaks in a Working Population: 2. Blood Pressure." *American Journal of Public Health* 67 (1977), pp. 954–959.

Peters, R. K., Benson, H., and Porter, D. "Daily Relaxation Response Breaks in a Working Population: 1. Health, Performance and Well-Being." *American Journal of Public Health* 67 (1977), pp. 946–953.

Rogers, C. R. *On Being a Person: A Therapist's View of Psychotherapy.* Boston: Houghton Mifflin, 1961.

Stainbrook, G. L., Hoffman, J. W., and Benson, H. "Behavioral Therapies of Hypertension: Psychotherapy, Biofeedback, and Relaxation/Meditation." *International Review of Applied Psychology* 32 (1983), pp. 119–135.

Wallace, R. K., and Benson, H. "The Physiology of Meditation." *Scientific American* 226 (1972), pp. 84–90.

Wallace, R. K., Benson, H., and Wilson, A. F. "A Wakeful Hypometabolic Physiologic State." *American Journal of Physiology* 221 (1971), pp. 795–799.

Yerkes, R. M., and Dodson, J. D. "The Relation of Strength of Stimulus to Rapidity of Habit-Formation." *Journal of Comparative Neurology and Psychology* 18 (1908), pp. 459–482.

Zamarra, J. W. M., Besseghini, I., and Wittenberg, S. "The Effects of the Transcendental Meditation Program on the Exercise Performance of Patients with Angina Pectoris." In *Scientific Research on the Transcendental Meditation Program. Collected Papers,* Vol. I, eds. W. Orme-Johnson and J. T. Farrow, pp. 270–277. West Germany: MERU Press, 1977.

Chapter 9

The Holy Bible. Old and New Testaments in the King James Version. Nashville, New York: Regency Publishing House, 1970.

Benson, H., and Epstein, M. D. "The Placebo Effect—A Neglected Asset in the Care of Patients." *Journal of the American Medical Association* 232 (1975), pp. 1225–1227.

Benson, H., and McCallie, D. P., Jr. "Angina Pectoris and the Placebo Effect." *New England Journal of Medicine* 300 (1979), pp. 1424–1429.

Castiglioni, A. *A History of Medicine.* New York: Knopf, 1941.

Edwards, H. *Thirty Years a Spiritual Healer.* London: Jenkins, 1968.

Grad, B. "A Telekinetic Effect on Plant Growth." *International Journal of Parapsychology* 5 (1963), pp. 117–133.

Grad, B. "A Telekinetic Effect on Plant Growth. II. Experiments Involving Treatment of Saline in Stoppered Bottles." *International Journal of Parapsychology* 6 (1964), pp. 473–498.

Grad, B. "Healing by the Laying on of Hands; Review of Experiments and Implications." *Pastoral Psychology* 21 (1970), pp. 19–26.

Grad, B. "Some Biological Effects of the 'laying-on-of-hands': A Review of Experiments with Animals and Plants." *Journal of* the American Society for Psychical Research 59 (1965), pp. 95–127.

Grad, B. "The 'laying-on-of-hands': Implications for Psychotherapy, Gentling, and the Placebo Effect." *Journal of the American Society for Psychical Research* 61 (1967), pp. 286–305.

Grad, B., Cadaret, R. J., and Paul, G. I. "The Influence of an Unorthodox Method of Treatment of Wound Healing in Mice." *International Journal of Parapsychology* 3 (1961), pp. 5–24.

Hammond, S. *We Are All Healers.* New York: Ballantine Books, 1973.

Hippocrates. *Precepts,* Chapter 6. Cited by A. M. Burgess and A. M. Burgess, Jr., in "Caring for the Patient—A Thrice-Told Tale." *New England Journal of Medicine* 274 (1966), pp. 1241–1244.

Inglis, B. *Fringe Medicine.* London: Faber and Faber, 1964.

LeShan, L. *The Medium, the Mystic and the Physicist.* New York: Ballantine Books, 1975.

Index

Index

Blumberg, Dr. E. M., 79–80
Borysenko, Dr. Joan Z., 79, 81
Buddhism:
  Dalai Lama and, 33
  feats of religious faith, 20, 25,
    30–31
  focus words for, 110
  Magic and Mystery in Tibet on,
    30–31
  monks, *see* Monks, *gTum-mo*
    Yoga; *Lung gom-pa* Yoga
  philosophy of, 20, 23
  prayer position of, 112
  technique for relieving pain,
    131–32
Bultmann, Rudolph, 22

Cancer, 79–81, 130–31
  doctors who emphasize the positive
    and, 88
Cardiac problems, 130
Catholic Encyclopedia, 113
Chail, 156
Charles X, 148
Chest pains, *see* Angina pectoris
Chi, 100, 147
Child-parent relationship, 85
Chinese Communists, 32, 35
Cholesterol levels, 131
Christ, Jesus, 21, 112–13
Christianity, 30
  focus words for, 107–08
  prayer positions of, 112, 113
  science and, 20–23
Clovis I, 148
Computers compared to the mind,
  14
Convulsions, epidemic, 73
Cooper, Dr. Michael J., 131
"Coping skills," 80
Corgard®, 120
Cravens, Penny, 38

Creativity, 140–42
Cross-country skiing, 140
"Cuff neurosis," 129–30

*Daily Prayers with English Transla-
  tion* (Philips), 109
Dalai Lama, 32
  described, 33
  Geshe, 53
  meeting with, 33–37, 156, 157
  testing of monks and, 35–37,
    44–45, 54
  Tibetan medicine and, 36, 68
  in Upper Dharmsala, 44–45, 59
"Dancing manias," 72–73
Dancing Wu Li Masters, The
  (Zukav), 20, 23
David-Neal, Alexandra, 30–31, 61
Death during sleep, 11
Digitalis, 89–90
"Disturbed sleep," 11
Doctor-patient relationship, 85–101
  child-parent relationship, 85
  friend-patient relationship, 69–70,
    87
  healing and, 150
  laboratory tests and, 94
  positive attitude and, 85–86
  step one: If ill, don't hesitate to go
    to the doctor, 86–87
  step two: Find a supportive doctor
    whom you trust, 87–88
  step three: Go to a doctor who em-
    phasizes the positive, 88–89
  step four: Don't expect a prescrip-
    tion, 89–90
  step five: If drugs or surgery are
    prescribed, find out why, 90–96
  step six: Use the Relaxation Re-
    sponse regularly, 96–101
  Tibetan medicine and, 65–68
  "vogue therapy" and, 95

174

Index

Goldman, Dr. Ralph F., 38–39, 40
Grad, Dr. Bernard, 153–55
gTum-mo Yoga, 47–61, 158
  "bliss state" of, 53–54
  described, 34
  implications of, 49–50, 61
  measuring the effect of, 38–39
  monks, *see* Monks, *gTum-mo*
    Yoga
  rejection of, 63–64
  as religious rite, 47–48
  translation of, 48
  trek to practitioners of, 50–52
Guatemala, 69–70

Hadrian, Emperor, 147
Harvard University:
  Dalai Lama at, 33–37
  Medical School, 29, 38, 79, 81
Headaches, 125–26
Healing, 147–59
  of animals, 152–54, 158
  healers and, 150–52
  history of, 147–48
  most puzzling kind of, 152–59
  placebo effect and, 149–52
  of plants, 154–55, 158
  question of, 147–49
  Relaxation Response and, 149,
    150–52
  scientific measurement of, 155–56
  self-willed, 149
Heartbeat and cardiac problems, 130
High blood pressure, 91–92, 128–30
Hinduism, 30
  focus words for, 110
Hippocrates, 12, 150
Holmes, Oliver Wendell, 89
Hopkins, Dr. Jeffrey, 38, 44, 45, 54
Hormones, 97
  counteracting, 99
  uses of, 98–99

Hypertension, 91–92, 128–30
Hyperventilation, 122–24

Imhotep, 147
Incarnation, 21–22
Inderal®, 120
India, 32, 42–43
  described, 39–40
  see also Upper Dharmsala
Inglis, Brian, 151
"Inhalation sickness," 73–74
Insomnia, 133–36
Israel, 64, 71

James, William, 33
Jogging, 129, 136–38
Journal of Human Stress, 131
Judaism, 30
  focus words for, 108–09
  prayer position of, 112
"Jumpers," 73

Ka, 100, 147
Karma between doctor and patient,
    36, 68
Khampas, 31
Khellin, 77–78
"King's touch," 147–48

"Laying on of hands," 147–48
  "Mr. E" and, 153–55
Lawrence of Arabia, 3–4, 10
Lehmann, Dr. John W., 38
LeShan, Lawrence, 151
Levitation, 20, 30–31
  demonstration of, 156–58
  Wallace on, 41
Lhasa, 53, 57, 58

Index

Index